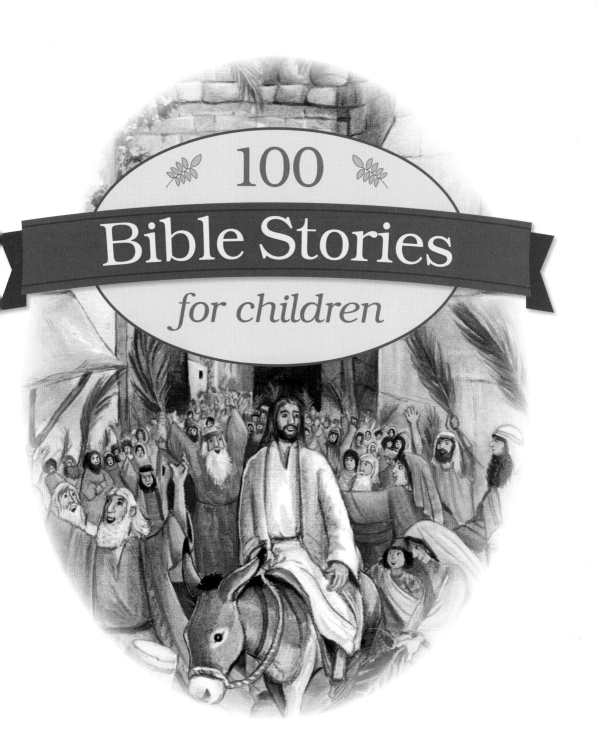

100 Bible Stories
for children

Tyndale House Publishers, Inc.
Carol Stream, Illinois

Visit Tyndale's website for kids at www.tyndale.com/kids.

TYNDALE is a registered trademark of Tyndale House Publishers, Inc.

The Tyndale Kids logo is a trademark of Tyndale House Publishers, Inc.

100 Bible Stories for Children

Copyright © 2018 by Tyndale House Publishers, Inc. All rights reserved.

Originally published under the title *Children's Bible in 100 Stories* by Copenhagen Publishing House, Denmark. First printing by Tyndale House Publishers, Inc., in 2018.

Illustrations by Gill Guile. Copyright © by Copenhagen Publishing House. All rights reserved.

For manufacturing information regarding this product, please call 1-800-323-9400.

For information about special discounts for bulk purchases, please contact Tyndale House Publishers at csresponse@tyndale.com, or call 1-800-323-9400.

Library of Congress Cataloging-in-Publication Data

Names: Tyndale House Publishers.

Title: 100 Bible stories for children.

Other titles: One hundred Bible stories for children.

Description: Carol Stream, Illinois : Tyndale House Publishers, Inc., 2018.

Identifiers: LCCN 2017047402 | ISBN 9781496431608 (hc)

Subjects: LCSH: Bible stories, English.

Classification: LCC BS551.3 .A15 2018 | DDC 220.95/05—dc23 LC record available at https://lccn.loc.gov/2017047402

Printed in China

24 23 22 21 20 19 18
7   6   5   4   3   2   1

Contents

NEW TESTAMENT

Old Testament

1

God Makes Everything

Genesis 1:1–2:3

In the beginning, God made the heavens and earth, but they were dark and empty. God, who has always been, said, "Let there be light!" And light suddenly appeared. God called the light day and separated it from the darkness, which he called night. That was the very first day.

Then God said, "Let there be a sky!" And so he made the big, blue sky. Night passed, and morning came. That was the second day.

Then God collected water into oceans and made dry land. He said, "Let plants grow from the earth." Out of the ground sprouted flowers, trees, and grass. That was the end of day three.

God wasn't done making things! On the fourth day, he said, "Let there be lights in my sky." He made the sun to shine during the day and the moon to glow at night. He hung all the stars in the sky and made each one sparkle.

On the fifth day, God said, "Let there be birds to fly in the air and fish to swim in the sea!" The water was soon filled with all kinds of wonderful swimming creatures. Up in the air, birds of all sizes soared, swooped, and fluttered.

On the sixth day, God made animals of all kinds to walk on earth—everything from tiny bugs to giant elephants. But God was still not done creating! God made human beings: a man and a woman. They were his most special creation, because they were made in his image.

God was very happy with everything he had made. "This is very good," he said.

The seventh day came, and God finally stopped working. He made this day special and set it apart for himself and his people to enjoy everything he had made.

2
Adam's Helper

Genesis 2:7-9, 18-25

Out of everything God created—on the earth, under the water, and up in the sky—human beings were the most special and important. God made them in his image, to take care of his wonderful world.

To make the very first man, God took dust from the ground and shaped it. God breathed life into the man, and he came alive. God named him Adam.

God planted a beautiful garden to be Adam's home. It was called the Garden of Eden. The trees in the garden were full of sweet, juicy fruit for Adam to eat.

Then God said, "It's not good for Adam to be by himself. I will make the perfect helper for him." God brought all the animals to Adam, and Adam gave them each a name. But none of the animals was the right helper for Adam.

So God made Adam fall into a deep sleep. God took a rib from Adam's side and made it into a woman. God brought her to Adam. Adam was so happy! "At last!" he said. "Here is the perfect partner for me!" Adam named the woman Eve.

Adam and Eve were very happy in the Garden of Eden. God had made it just for them, and it was the perfect place for them to be.

3

The Fall

Genesis 2:16-17; 3:1-13, 20-24

In the middle of the Garden of Eden, God had
planted the tree of the knowledge of good and evil.
"You may eat the fruit from any tree in the Garden
except for this one," God said.

God had an enemy called Satan. Satan entered the
Garden in the form of a snake and slithered up to
Eve. "Is it true that God said that you must not eat
fruit from any tree in the Garden?" he said.

Eve answered, "God told us we may eat fruit from

all the trees here, except from the tree in the middle of the Garden. We should not even touch it or we'll die." The snake said, "God is lying to you. If you eat this fruit, you will be like God, and he doesn't want that to happen."

Eve listened to what the snake said and looked at the fruit. "It must be tasty," she thought. So she picked a piece of fruit from the tree of the knowledge of good and evil and tasted it, and she gave another one to Adam, and he tasted it as well. After eating the fruit, Adam and Eve immediately felt ashamed. They had done the one thing God had told them not to do. They also realized for the first time that they were naked. They decided to sew fig leaves together to cover their bodies.

That evening, God walked in the Garden and called out for Adam, "Where are you?" Adam answered, "I'm hiding from you because I'm naked." God asked him, "How did you know that you were naked? Did you eat the fruit from the tree that I told you not to eat from?" Adam replied, "Eve made me eat it." God turned to Eve and asked, "What did you do?" She answered, "The snake tricked me."

Because of their disobedience, Adam and Eve were thrown out of the Garden of Eden. But God still loved them. Before they left, God made them clothes from animal skins.

4

Cain and Abel

Genesis 4:1-15

After they left the Garden of Eden, Adam and Eve had a son they named Cain. Later on, they had another son, Abel. When the brothers grew up, Abel became a shepherd while Cain became a farmer.

One day Cain and Abel brought gifts to God. Cain brought some of the crops from his farm. Abel brought the best lamb from his flock. God accepted Abel's gift but not Cain's. This made Cain very angry.

God asked Cain, "Why are you angry? If you do the right thing, I will be pleased with you. Be careful, because if you don't do what is right, sin will attack you. Sin wants to control you, but you must rule over it."

But Cain's heart was already filled with hatred for his brother. He said, "Abel, let's go out into the field." When they got there, Cain attacked Abel and killed him. Nobody saw what happened. At least that's what Cain thought.

But God said to Cain, "Where is Abel?"

Cain answered, "How should I know? It's not my job to take care of my brother."

God replied, "What did you do? Your brother's blood is calling to me from the ground!" The Lord continued, "You will now be cursed. Even when you work hard, the ground will not grow good crops for you. You will have to spend your days wandering around the earth."

Cain cried out to God because he was afraid that any person who met him would kill him. So God put a mark on Cain to warn people not to kill him.

5

Noah and the Ark

Genesis 6:5–7:16

The earth was filled with more and more people, and they chose to do worse and worse things. When God saw how evil people's actions and thoughts had become, he felt sorry for ever making them. He decided to get rid of everything and everyone.

Out of all the people on earth, there was one person who was good. His name was Noah, and he listened to God and obeyed him. God shared his plans with Noah. "I want you to make an ark, a huge boat made of wood. There will be a flood that will destroy every living thing on the earth, but I will keep you and your family safe. Bring a pair of each animal, a male and female, inside the ark. Bring seven pairs of each clean animal. Store food for your family and the animals to eat."

Noah did everything that the Lord wanted him to do. Day after day, Noah worked to build the ark. He followed God's instructions carefully. After working on the ark for many years, Noah finally finished it. God said, "It is time for you to enter the ark with your family and all the animals. Soon the rain will start to fall." Noah, his wife, their three sons, and their sons' wives went into the ark, along with all the animals. God shut the door behind them as the rain began to fall from the sky.

6

The Flood

Genesis 7:17–8:12

Rain fell without stopping for 40 days and nights. The water rose higher and higher until it covered the whole earth, even the tallest mountains. The Flood covered the earth for 150 days.

Then God commanded the wind to blow, and the floodwaters started to go down. Finally, the ark rested on the mountains of Ararat—but Noah and his family and the animals could not leave the ark until the land was dry again. Noah's family and the animals waited and waited. After months of waiting, Noah opened the window of the ark and released a raven. It flew back and forth over the water, but it couldn't find any dry land, so it had to come back to the ark. Then Noah sent out another bird—a dove. The dove couldn't find any dry land to perch on, so it came back too. After another week passed, Noah sent out the dove again. This time it came back with an olive leaf in its beak.

After another week went by Noah sent out the dove again. He waited and waited for the bird to come back to the ark, but it didn't. Noah knew that soon the land would be dry.

7
God's Promise
Genesis 8:13–9:17

Noah, his family, and all the animals waited a long, long time to leave the ark. One day, more than 10 months after the Flood began, Noah looked out of the ark and saw that there was no more water on the ground. Two months later, the ground was completely dry! God told Noah, "You and your family may leave the ark now. Let out the animals, too." Noah and his family were so excited and thankful to step out of the ark onto dry land!

Noah built an altar to worship and thank God for saving him and his family from the Flood. God was happy with what Noah did, and he made a promise to Noah and his family: "I will never again destroy everything living on the earth by sending a flood. You and the people after you can count on my promise." God blessed Noah and his sons and told them to have children and take care of the earth. "Here is the sign of my promise," God said. He made a beautiful rainbow appear in the sky. "Whenever you see the rainbow," God said, "remember that I will not flood the whole earth ever again."

8

The Tower of Babel

Genesis 11:1-9

There was a time when all people in the world spoke only one language. They all lived together and decided to build a city.

"Let's fill our city with big, beautiful buildings," the people said. "We'll build a tall, tall tower that reaches all the way up to the sky. This will make us famous and keep us together in this place."

God came and saw what the people were doing. He saw how proud they had become and how they wanted to take care of themselves without paying attention to God or asking for his help. God said, "This tower is just the beginning. What will these people do next? Nothing will stop them!"

God decided to mix up the people's speech so they couldn't understand each other. This made it hard for them to continue building together, and finally they gave up building the tower and the city. They separated and moved to different places. The city was later called Babel.

9

Abram's Faith
in the Lord

Genesis 11:27–12:5

Once there was a rich man named Abram. He lived in a city called Ur, where most people worshiped fake gods called idols. But Abram followed the one true God. One day, God said to Abram, "Leave your country and go to a place I will show you. I will make you into a great nation and make you famous. I will bless those who bless you and curse those who curse you. All the peoples on earth will be blessed through you."

Abram was 75 years old when God called him, but he had no children. Still, he had faith in God and his promises, so he did what God told him to do. He packed up all of his things and left his home country. His wife, Sarai, and his nephew Lot went with him. Abram didn't have a map, and he didn't know where or when his journey would end. But he trusted God and followed him every step of the way.

10
The Visit

Genesis 17:1-6, 15-16; 18:1-14

God promised Abram that he would have many descendants. He changed Abram's name to Abraham, which means "father of many." God also gave Abraham's wife, Sarai, a new name: Sarah, which means "princess."

Abraham and his family traveled often, moving whenever God told them to, so they lived in tents instead of houses. One day, while Abraham was sitting near the entrance to his tent, he saw three men coming toward him. He ran to meet them and offered to give them some food. The men rested under a tree while Abraham and Sarah prepared a meal for them. While the visitors ate, Abraham stood near them to make sure they had everything they wanted.

The visitors asked Abraham, "Where is your wife, Sarah?"

"She is in the tent," Abraham answered.

One of the men said, "I will come back in a year, and by then, you and Sarah will have a son."

Sarah was listening to the men from her tent. She overheard this and laughed. She thought, "I'm too old to have a child."

God said to Abraham, "Why did Sarah laugh and doubt that you will have a baby? Nothing is too hard for me! I tell you that at this time next year, you and Sarah will have a son."

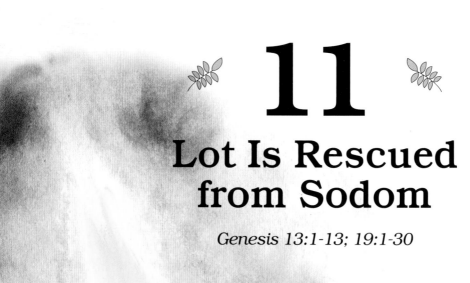

11

Lot Is Rescued from Sodom

Genesis 13:1-13; 19:1-30

Abraham and his nephew Lot each owned many animals. They decided to move away from each other to make sure that there was enough grass and water for their animals. Lot eventually moved to a city named Sodom. Sodom was full of people who did terrible things. There was so much evil in the city that God decided to destroy it. But first, two angels came to visit the city, and Lot invited them to his house. The two angels agreed to come, and Lot prepared a feast for them.

That night, evil men from the city came and surrounded Lot's house. They pounded on the door and shouted, "Lot, bring out your guests!"

Lot went outside to talk to the men. "Leave my guests alone," he begged them. "I have promised to protect them. Go away!"

But the men from the city would not leave. "Get out of our way!" they yelled at Lot. They rushed at Lot, trying to break down the door.

The two angels saw what was happening and pulled Lot back inside the house and locked the door. Then they made the men of Sodom blind to keep them from finding the door. The angels told Lot that he needed to get out of the city with his family before it was destroyed. "Run out of the city and don't look back!" the angels told Lot and his family.

Lot, his wife, and their two daughters ran out of Sodom. The Lord made fire and burning sulfur fall on Sodom and a nearby city, Gomorrah, destroying them. As Lot's family ran away from Sodom, Lot's wife looked back. She instantly turned into a pillar of salt. Lot and his two daughters kept running and went to live in a cave in the mountains.

12

Isaac

Genesis 21:1-7; 22:1-14

God kept his promise to Abraham and Sarah.
They had a son and named him Isaac, which means
"laughter." They both loved Isaac very much. As Isaac
grew, his parents loved him more and more every day.

One day God tested Abraham to see if Abraham
loved Isaac or God more.

"Abraham," God called out.

"Yes, Lord," Abraham replied.

"Take your only son and go to the land of Moriah. I want you to sacrifice him as an offering to me."

Early the next morning, Abraham got up and took Isaac and two of his servants with him. They traveled for a long time. On the third day, Abraham told his servants to stay with the donkey while he and Isaac continued on their way.

Isaac was puzzled. "Father, where is the lamb for the sacrifice?"

Abraham replied, "The Lord will provide it, Son."

When they arrived where God had told Abraham to go, Abraham built an altar and got it ready for the sacrifice. He took Isaac in his arms and laid him on the altar. Abraham lifted his knife, but just then the angel of the Lord said, "Abraham! Abraham! Stop! Don't harm your son! I now know that you will trust and obey me completely."

Abraham heard a sound in a nearby bush and saw a ram caught there by its horns. He took the ram and sacrificed it on the altar instead of Isaac. Abraham named that place "God provides" because God saved Isaac's life and provided an animal for the offering.

13
Esau and Jacob

Genesis 25:20-34

When Isaac grew up, he married a woman named
Rebekah. They could not have children, so Isaac
prayed for his wife. God answered his prayer, and
Rebekah got pregnant—with twin babies!

When it was time for Rebekah to have her babies,
the first to be born was red and hairy. Isaac and

Rebekah named him Esau. The second baby was born holding on to his brother's heel. Isaac and Rebekah named him Jacob.

The boys grew up liking different things. Esau loved to hunt while Jacob chose to stay at home most of the time. Their father, Isaac, loved Esau most while their mother loved Jacob most.

One day, when Esau came home from hunting, he found Jacob cooking stew. Esau said to his brother, "Give me some of that stew, Jacob. I am so hungry!"

Jacob told Esau, "I will only give you some food if you will give me your rights as the oldest son."

Esau agreed and sold his special rights to Jacob for a bowl of stew.

14

Jacob Steals a Blessing

Genesis 27:1-45

Many years later, Isaac's eyesight became so bad that he was almost blind. He told Esau, "Hunt for some meat and cook my favorite dish. Afterward, I will give you the blessing of the firstborn son."

Rebekah overheard this and called for her other son, Jacob. "Get two goats from our flock, and I will make your father's favorite dish. Take it to your father so that he will bless you instead of Esau."

"But Father will know it's me!" Jacob said. "Esau has hairy skin, and my skin is smooth."

"Just do as I tell you," Rebekah replied.

Rebekah took some of Esau's clothes and told Jacob to put them on. She covered Jacob's arms and neck with the hairy skin of the goats. When the food was ready, she told Jacob to take it to Isaac.

Jacob went to Isaac, carrying the delicious food. "Father?" he said.

"Which one are you, Esau or Jacob?" Isaac asked.

"It's Esau, Father, your oldest son," Jacob lied. "I have the food you asked for."

Isaac asked, "How were you able to get the meat so quickly?"

Jacob lied again. "God helped me."

Isaac asked Jacob to come closer. "Let me make sure it is really you, Esau." Isaac ran his hand over Jacob's arm and felt the hairy goatskin.

One more time, Isaac asked him, "Are you really Esau?"

"Yes, Father, it is really me, Esau," Jacob said.

Jacob gave Isaac the meal his mother had prepared. After he ate, Isaac asked Jacob to kiss him. When Jacob kissed him, Isaac smelled Esau's clothes, which Jacob was wearing. Then Isaac was convinced that it was really Esau.

So Isaac blessed Jacob. Soon after Jacob left Isaac, Esau arrived. Isaac trembled when he realized that Jacob had tricked him.

Esau was very angry that Jacob had stolen his blessing, so angry that he said he wanted to kill his brother. So Rebekah told Jacob to leave home and go stay with his uncle Laban for a while.

15

Jacob's Dream

Genesis 28:10-22

It was a long journey to Laban's house, and Jacob had to stop on the way. He lay down to sleep, using a stone as a pillow. Jacob dreamed of a stairway from earth reaching up to heaven, and he saw angels going up and down it. He saw God standing at the top of the stairway. God said, "I am the Lord, the God of your grandfather Abraham and your father, Isaac. I will give you and your children and your children's children the land on which you are lying. People will be blessed through you and your children. I will watch over you, and I will always be with you."

When Jacob woke up, he thought, "God lives here! This is the gate to heaven!" He got up early the next morning and set his stone pillow upright and made a memorial pillar. He poured olive oil over it and named the place Bethel, which means "house of God." He promised God, "If you will take care of me and provide me with everything that I need for my journey, and keep me safe until I return to my father, then you will be my God."

16

An Angry Brother Forgives

Genesis 31:3; 32:1–33:11

Twenty years later, Jacob had his own family. One day, God told him that it was time to go back to the land where he grew up. Jacob knew he would have to see his brother, Esau, again. So he sent a messenger ahead of him to tell Esau, "Jacob wants you to know that he has been living with your uncle Laban, and now he has many animals and servants. He is coming

to see you." When the messengers returned to Jacob, they told him that Esau would be meeting him with an army of 400 men.

Jacob prayed to the Lord, "God, help me! Save me from Esau's anger, because I am afraid he will come and attack me and my family. Remember that you promised to bless and protect me and my family."

Jacob sent some servants ahead of him with gifts of many animals for Esau, hoping that the gifts would help Esau forgive him. While Jacob was waiting in his camp, a mysterious man came and wrestled with him. The two of them wrestled all night long, until the dawn. The man touched Jacob's hip and hurt it, but Jacob wouldn't let go of the man until he blessed him. The man asked Jacob, "What is your name?"

"My name is Jacob," he replied.

"Your name will no longer be Jacob," the man said. "Instead it will be Israel, meaning 'God-Wrestler.'" Then the man blessed Jacob. Later on, Jacob realized that he had wrestled with God. He named the place Peniel, which means "the face of God."

Afterward, Jacob saw Esau coming with his 400 men. He bowed down to the ground seven times as he approached his brother. Esau ran to Jacob and hugged him tight. They both cried tears of joy. Jacob introduced his whole family to his brother. "Please accept my gifts, Esau," Jacob said. "The Lord has blessed me, and I'd like to share what I have with you."

Jacob was so happy. His brother who had been so angry had finally forgiven him.

17

Joseph the Dreamer

Genesis 37:1-11

Jacob lived in the land of Canaan with his 12 sons. Jacob loved one of his sons, Joseph, more than all the others. Jacob made a beautiful robe especially for Joseph. Joseph's older brothers were angry that he was their father's favorite. They didn't even want to speak to Joseph.

Things got worse when Joseph started telling his brothers about his dreams. Joseph said to them, "We were binding bundles of grain out in the fields when my bundle stood up straight. All of your bundles gathered around my bundle and bowed down to it."

"What are you saying?" his brothers asked. "Do you think you are going to be king over us?"

Their anger didn't stop Joseph from telling them about another dream. In this dream, the sun, the moon, and 11 stars were bowing down to him.

This time Jacob was upset also. He scolded Joseph and said, "What kind of dream is that, Joseph? Will I, your mother, and your brothers actually bow down to you?" But Jacob thought about what Joseph's dreams could mean.

18

Joseph Is Sold by His Brothers

Genesis 37:12-36

One day, while Joseph's brothers were out in the fields watching their sheep, Jacob asked Joseph to check on them. When Joseph's brothers saw him coming, they said, "Our little brother, the dreamer, is coming! Why don't we kill him and just say that a wild animal ate him?" When Reuben, the oldest brother, heard this, he said, "There's no need to kill him. Let's just throw him into this dry well!" He said

this because he wanted to come back later and rescue Joseph from the well.

When Joseph met his brothers, they took off his beautiful robe that his father had given him and threw him down in the empty well. As the brothers were eating, they saw a group of traders on their way to Egypt. One of the brothers, Judah, said, "Why don't we just sell Joseph to the traders? That way we'll get some money and we won't need to kill him. After all, he's still our brother." The brothers agreed and sold Joseph to the traders.

Reuben wasn't there when the brothers sold Joseph. When he came back to rescue Joseph from the well, Reuben was very upset to find that Joseph was gone. "What will we do now?" he asked his brothers.

The brothers got Joseph's robe, killed a goat, and dipped Joseph's robe in the blood. When they returned to their father, they showed him the blood-stained robe. They said, "We found this. Do you think this is Joseph's robe?"

Jacob couldn't believe his eyes. "Some wild animal must have eaten Joseph!" he said. Jacob was very sad. When his children tried to make him feel better, he said, "I will be sad until the day I die."

Jacob did not know that Joseph had been sold to Potiphar, an official of Pharaoh, the king of Egypt.

19

Joseph in Prison

Genesis 39:1–41:40

Joseph did a very good job serving Potiphar, and God blessed everything Potiphar owned because of Joseph. Potiphar trusted Joseph and put him in charge of his entire house and all the other servants.

Joseph was also very handsome, and Potiphar's wife began to pay lots of attention to him. "Let's spend time together, Joseph. Just the two of us," she said. But Joseph knew that this would be wrong.

"My master, Potiphar, trusts me," Joseph said. "You are his wife, and it would be wrong of me to act as if you were mine. I do not want to do such an evil thing and sin against God."

Potiphar's wife tried to change Joseph's mind, but he stayed away from her. One day she finally got Joseph alone, but he ran away so fast that he left his cloak with her. Potiphar's wife got very angry with Joseph for not doing what she wanted, so she screamed as loudly as she could. When her servants came running to see what was wrong, she lied, saying that Joseph had tried to hurt her. When Potiphar heard her story, he became furious with Joseph and threw him in prison.

But God was with Joseph even in prison. The

warden liked Joseph and put him in charge of the other prisoners.

Some time later, Pharaoh's chief cupbearer and chief baker were also put in prison. One night they each had dreams that worried them. With God's help, Joseph told the two men what their dreams meant. The baker was going to be killed by Pharaoh, but the cupbearer would soon be let out of prison. Joseph told the cupbearer, "Please ask Pharaoh to help me, because I haven't done anything wrong." Three days later, the chief cupbearer got his old job back in Pharaoh's palace, but he forgot all about Joseph.

Two years later, Pharaoh had two very upsetting dreams, and none of his advisers could tell him what they meant. Then the chief cupbearer finally remembered Joseph and told Pharaoh about him. Pharaoh immediately sent for Joseph.

Joseph explained to Pharaoh that he could tell what dreams mean only because God helped him. Pharaoh then shared his two dreams, one of seven thin cows eating seven fat cows, and the other of seven thin heads of grain eating seven healthy heads. Joseph said, "Your two dreams have the same meaning. There will be seven years of very good harvests, followed by seven years of famine. Save food from the years of good crops to eat during the years of no crops. Put a wise man in charge over the land of Egypt to make sure that you are prepared."

Pharaoh could see that Joseph was filled with God's Spirit. He said, "There is no one wiser than you. I will put you in charge of my kingdom. I will be the only one who is greater than you."

20

Joseph's Brothers Go to Egypt

Genesis 42:1–45:28

Everything Joseph had said to Pharaoh
happened. There were seven years of good crops,
during which there was more than enough food. Then
the seven years of famine came. Because of Joseph's
preparations, there was plenty of food in Egypt, but in
the land of Canaan, where Jacob still lived with his
other sons, there was no food. So Jacob asked his
sons to go to Egypt to buy food. When the 10 brothers
arrived, they bowed down to the governor of Egypt—
Joseph! Joseph recognized his brothers, but they
didn't know who he was. "You're spies from Canaan!"
Joseph said.

"No!" his brothers replied. "We are here to buy food.
We are all brothers. There used to be 12 of us, but
one stayed with our father, and one is not with us
anymore."

To prove who they were, Joseph asked them to
bring him their youngest brother while another
brother, Simeon, stayed behind. Joseph ordered his
servants to fill his brothers' sacks with grain and to
put the silver they had paid for the grain back in their

sacks. On their journey back home the brothers found the silver. They worried that the governor might think that they had stolen it.

When the food ran out, Jacob asked them to go back to Egypt to buy more, but his sons told him that they could not return to Egypt without their youngest brother, Benjamin. Jacob did not want to lose one more son, but Judah promised him that he would take care of Benjamin, and Jacob finally let them go.

When they returned to Egypt, Joseph not only sold them more food but invited them to eat at his house. The brothers were amazed to see that he seated them at the table from oldest to youngest. When it was time for them to leave, Joseph again asked the servants to put the silver back in his brothers' sacks and to put his own silver cup in Benjamin's sack.

As the brothers headed home, Joseph's servants ran after them. "Why did you steal my master's special cup?" the palace manager demanded.

The brothers said, "If you find anything stolen in our things, the one who took it will be killed, and the rest of us will become the governor's slaves."

They were horrified when Joseph's cup was found in Benjamin's sack. They all went back to Joseph's house. Judah told Joseph that they would now all be his slaves.

Joseph replied, "No, only the man who has stolen the cup will become my slave."

Judah begged him, "Our father will die if Benjamin is not with us when we return. Let me stay instead to take his place."

Joseph couldn't keep his secret any longer. He said, "I am your brother Joseph! It was not you but God who sent me here to Egypt to save many people's lives."

The brothers threw their arms around each other and cried. Eventually Joseph's brothers and their families moved to Egypt, where they lived for many years.

21

A Baby in a Basket

Exodus 1:6–2:10; 6:20

Many years later, the descendants of Joseph and his brothers were called the Israelites. They still lived in Egypt, but the pharaoh who ruled the land didn't remember what Joseph had done for his country. He was worried that the Israelites would try to take over the land of Egypt, so he made them work as slaves. The Israelites had to work very hard all day long for no pay. But every day there were more and more Israelites, and Pharaoh was still scared that they would fight against him. So Pharaoh ordered that every baby boy born to the Israelites should be thrown into the Nile River.

An Israelite couple named Amram and Jochebed had a baby boy during this time. They saw that he was a special baby, and they hid him for three months. But they could not hide him forever, so

Jochebed got a basket and covered it with tar and pitch. Jochebed put her baby gently in the basket and placed it in the tall grass by the edge of the river. Miriam, the baby's big sister, watched him from a distance.

Pharaoh's daughter came down to the river to take a bath. The princess saw the basket and asked her servants to bring it to her. When she opened the basket, she was surprised to see a baby inside! He was crying, and the princess felt sorry for him. "This is a little Israelite boy," she said.

Miriam walked up to the princess and said, "Do you want me to call one of the Israelite women to nurse and take care of this baby for you?" The princess agreed, and Miriam brought her own mother to the princess.

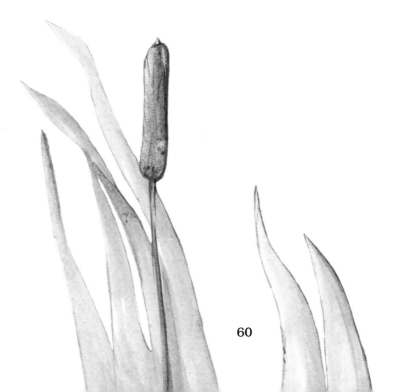

Pharaoh's daughter promised to pay Jochebed to nurse the baby for her. When the child was old enough, Jochebed brought him to the princess, who adopted him as her own son. The princess named him Moses, which means, "I pulled him out of the water."

22

Moses Flees Egypt

Exodus 2:11-21; 3:1

Even though Moses grew up in the palace as the
son of the princess, he went out to watch his people,
the Israelites. One day, he saw an Egyptian beating
an Israelite. Moses looked around to make sure no
one could see him, then he killed the Egyptian. He
hid the Egyptian's body in the sand. The next day,
when he was visiting the Israelite slaves again, he saw
an Israelite man beating another Israelite. "Why are
you treating your friend that way?" Moses asked him.

The man replied, "Do you think you are our prince
and our judge? Are you going to kill me like you killed
that Egyptian yesterday?"

Moses was terrified. "Everyone knows what I did!"
he said. When Pharaoh heard what had happened, he
tried to kill Moses. Moses ran far away to a land
called Midian. There he met and married a woman
named Zipporah. Moses became a shepherd, helping
his father-in-law, Jethro.

23

Moses and the Burning Bush

Exodus 3:1–4:17

One day Moses was taking care of his sheep in the desert. Suddenly, he saw a fire in a bush. But this was no ordinary fire, because it didn't burn the bush up. When he went to get a closer look he heard a voice calling, "Moses! Moses!"

"Here I am!" Moses said.

"Don't come any closer!" said the voice. "Take off your shoes. This is holy ground. I am the God of Abraham, Isaac, and Jacob." Moses covered his face because he was afraid to look at God.

God said, "My people in Egypt have been suffering, and I have heard their cries for help. It is time to set them free from the Egyptians and lead them to a beautiful land that I will give them. I am going to send you to Pharaoh, and you must tell him to let my people go."

"I don't think I can do it," Moses replied. "I am not good enough."

"I will be with you," God told him.

Moses was still worried. "What if no one believes you have sent me?" he asked.

God gave Moses two miracle signs to show the people. He turned Moses' staff into a snake and then back into a staff. He also made one of Moses' hands diseased and then healed it instantly. But Moses was still worried.

"I am not good at talking, God," he said.

"I will tell you what to say," God replied.

"Please, send someone else," Moses begged.

"I will send your brother, Aaron, to you," God said. "He will speak for you."

Finally, Moses obeyed God and went back to Egypt.

24

The Ten Plagues

Exodus 7:1–12:30

Moses and his brother, Aaron, went to the palace to tell Pharaoh to let the Israelites go. "No!" Pharaoh said to Moses and Aaron. "I will not let your people go."

The Lord told Moses, "Go to Pharaoh and tell him that until he lets the Israelites go, bad things will happen to Egypt. Then he will know that I am the real God."

Again and again, Moses told Pharaoh to let the Israelites go, and again and again, Pharaoh said, "No!" Every time Pharaoh said no, God sent a terrible plague on Egypt.

With the first plague, God turned the water of the great Nile River into blood. With the second plague, frogs suddenly appeared everywhere. The frogs croaked every minute of every day. But still Pharaoh would not let the Israelites go.

For the third plague, dust turned into gnats. The gnats covered all the people and animals in Egypt.

Plague number four was just as bad. Huge swarms of flies covered the city. For the fifth plague, the Egyptians' animals got very sick and died. One by one, they fell to the ground.

During the sixth plague, terrible sores covered the Egyptians and the animals that were left.

For the seventh plague, God sent a gigantic storm of thunder and hail. The eighth plague was locusts. A blanket of locusts covered the land and ate the food that was growing on the people's farms.

The ninth plague was thick, deep darkness. For three days and nights, nobody could see anything. But God took care of his people by making sure that there was light where the Israelites lived.

After all this, Pharaoh still would not let the Israelites go. So God told Moses he would send one last terrible plague. An angel would pass through Egypt in the middle of the night and would kill every firstborn son. But God also told Moses that the Israelites should mark their doors with the blood of a lamb.

The angel did not go into any of the houses where there was blood on the door. But the firstborn son of every Egyptian family died, including Pharaoh's own son.

25

The Passover Meal

Exodus 12:1-28

Before God sent the tenth plague, he gave instructions to his people about a special meal. He sent Moses and Aaron to tell the Israelites what was going to happen and what they needed to do to be safe.

First, the Israelites should get a perfect one-year-old lamb and kill it. They should take some of the lamb's blood and put it on the sides and the top of the door frame of their houses. They should roast the meat that same night and eat it with bitter herbs and bread made without yeast.

God told his people what they should wear during this meal. He told them to wear clothes for traveling and to carry a staff.

God told the Israelites that every year from that day on, each family in the Israelite community should share this special meal. He called this meal the Passover to remember the time when he passed over the people of Israel and did not kill their firstborn sons.

26

The Crossing of the Red Sea

Exodus 12:31-42; 13:17–14:31

After the death of the firstborn sons of Egypt, Pharaoh told Moses and Aaron, "Go! Get out of Egypt, and take all of your people with you." The Israelites packed all their things and left as fast as they could. For 430 years, the Israelites had lived in Egypt as slaves. Now they were finally free and headed for the land God had promised them.

God led the people through the desert toward the Red Sea. During the day, the Lord went ahead of the Israelites in a pillar of cloud and at night, in a pillar of fire. God never left his people.

Back in Egypt, Pharaoh changed his mind about letting the Israelites go. He gathered his soldiers, chariots, and weapons and chased after the Israelites. When the Israelites saw the Egyptian army coming, they were very afraid. "Lord, what are we going to do? There is no escape! The Egyptians are behind us and the Red Sea is in front of us." They told Moses, "Why did we have to leave Egypt? It's better to be slaves than to die here in the wilderness."

Moses told them, "Do not be afraid. The Lord will rescue us and will fight for us."

God said to Moses, "Hold your staff over the water, and the sea will split and open up a path for you. You will walk through the sea on dry ground." Moses did as God said, and walls of water formed on each side of the Israelites as they walked on dry ground right through the Red Sea. As soon as the Israelites were safe, the Lord said to Moses, "Hold your staff over the sea again." The walls of water fell on Pharaoh and his army. God had rescued his people from the Egyptians!

27

God Takes Care of His People in the Desert

Exodus 16:1–17:7

The Israelites traveled through the desert for a long time, and there wasn't much food for them to eat. "Why did God bring us into this desert?" the people complained. "What good is being free when we are so hungry?"

The Lord told Moses, "I am going to send down food from heaven for you. You will have all the bread and meat you can eat. Then the people will know that I am really God."

That evening, the camp was covered with quail that the people could catch and eat. The next morning, there was a layer of dew around the camp, which turned into white flakes of bread. The Israelites called it manna.

As the people traveled around, they came to a place where they couldn't find any water to drink. The people complained again. "Give us water!" they yelled at Moses. Moses asked God for help, and the Lord

told him, "Take your staff and strike the rock at Mount Sinai." Moses did as he was told, and water poured out of the rock. There was plenty of water for all the Israelites to drink.

28

The Ten Commandments

Exodus 19:1–20:17

While the Israelites were at Mount Sinai, God told Moses that he would be giving his people instructions that they needed to follow. God wanted his people to know how to live the right way so that he could live with them. The Israelites promised that they would listen and do what God said.

Moses climbed to the top of the mountain while the people stayed at the bottom. The whole mountain trembled and was covered with smoke as God came down on it in fire. God gave Moses a special set of rules called the Ten Commandments.

1. I am your God, who rescued you from slavery in Egypt. You must not have any other god except for me.
2. Don't make any kind of idol to worship.
3. Only speak my name with respect.
4. Remember the Sabbath, my special day. Work for six days each week, but on the seventh day, rest. For I created everything in six days, but on the seventh day I rested.
5. Honor your father and mother. If you do this, you will have a long life.
6. Do not murder.
7. You must stay faithful to your spouse.
8. Do not steal.
9. Do not lie.
10. Do not let your heart want things that other people have.

29

The Golden Calf

Exodus 32:1-35

While God was talking to Moses up on the mountain, the people began to get impatient. "Why is Moses taking so long? Maybe he's not coming back. Make us some gods who can lead us instead," they told Aaron. Aaron told the people to give him their golden earrings, which he used to make an idol shaped like a calf. Aaron built an altar in front of the golden calf, and the next day the people had a big party to worship the idol.

Up on the mountain, God told Moses, "Go down and see what my people are doing. They have made a golden calf to worship."

Moses came down from the mountain holding the two stone tablets with the Ten Commandments written by God's hand. When he saw what the people were doing, he was so angry that he threw the stone tablets to the ground. He took the golden calf and burned it. He ground it into powder, mixed it with water, and forced the people to drink it. They repented and asked God to forgive them.

Moses stood at the entrance of the camp and said, "All of you who are on the Lord's side, join me." Many people did. As for the people who refused to join Moses, God punished them for disobeying him and worshiping the golden calf.

30

Twelve Spies

Numbers 13:1–14:35

God told Moses, "Choose a leader from each of the 12 tribes of Israel to go out and explore the land of Canaan."

Moses told the spies, "Tell me everything about the land. See if the land is good or bad, if the towns have walls, and if the people there are strong or weak. Also bring back some crops for us to see."

Forty days later, the spies returned and reported, "Canaan is a beautiful country, a land flowing with milk and honey. Look at the fruit we brought back! However, the people living there are very strong, and their towns are large, with thick walls."

One of the spies, Caleb, spoke up, "Let's go and conquer the land. We can do it!"

But the rest of the spies disagreed. "The people of the land are much stronger than we are! We cannot fight them."

The Israelites became afraid and said, "Why did God promise to give us a land we can't conquer?" They complained about Moses and Aaron and decided to choose somebody to lead them back to Egypt.

Caleb and another spy, Joshua, tried to encourage them by saying, "The land we traveled through is wonderful. If the Lord is happy with us, he will bring us there safely. Do not disobey God, and do not be afraid of the people of the land. The Lord is with us!"

God was happy with Caleb and Joshua's faith and told them that they would be the only spies allowed to enter the Promised Land. But first the Israelites would wander in the wilderness for 40 years, and everyone who was 20 years or older would die before that time was up as punishment for their lack of faith in God.

31

Snakes Everywhere

Numbers 20:14-21; 21:4-9

Because the Israelites did not trust God, he sent them back to wander in the desert for 40 years. But God continued to care for them.

The king of Edom would not let the Israelites walk through his land, so the Israelites had to go around. It was a long trip, and once again they began to complain. "Why did you have to take us out of Egypt?" they grumbled to Moses. "We're going to die of hunger and thirst here in the desert!"

As a punishment for their complaining, God sent poisonous snakes to bite the people. Many of the

Israelites died from the poisonous bites. The people realized that they had been wrong, and they said to Moses, "We should not have complained about God and about you. We are sorry! Please ask the Lord to take away the snakes!" Moses asked God to help the people.

God had mercy on his people and told Moses, "Make a snake out of bronze and attach it to a pole. Tell the people that if they get bitten, all they need to do is to look at the bronze snake and they will be healed." Moses did as God had said, and after that the people were healed from the snakebites just by looking at the bronze snake.

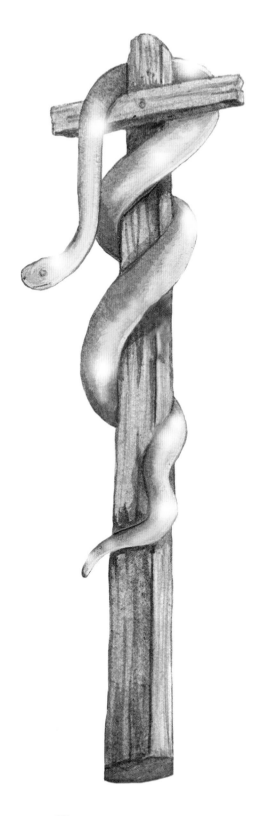

32

A New Leader for Israel

Deuteronomy 32:1-52; 34:1-12

The Israelites' 40 years of wandering in the desert were finally almost over. Moses gathered all of the people and reminded them of all the miracles God had done for them and of how he had taken care of them in the wilderness. Moses also instructed them to follow the Ten Commandments and to teach their children to carefully obey and trust the Lord.

God told Moses, "Climb up to the top of Mount Nebo. From there you will be able to see the Promised Land. Then you will die on the mountain." When Moses reached the top of the mountain, God said to him, "This is the land I promised to Abraham, Isaac, and Jacob, the land I said I would give to my people."

After Moses died, his assistant, Joshua, took his place as the leader of God's people. Joshua would be the one who finally led the Israelites into the Promised Land.

33

Rahab and the Spies

Joshua 2:1-24

It was time for the Israelites to enter the land of Canaan, the Promised Land. Joshua asked two men to spy on the land on the other side of the Jordan River, paying special attention to the city of Jericho. When the spies got to Jericho, they stayed at the house of a woman named Rahab. But someone noticed them and told the king of Jericho. The king sent some men to Rahab's house to capture the spies.

The king's men stomped into Rahab's house. They asked her, "Where are the men from Israel who came to you to stay in your house? They are spies!"

Rahab had hidden the spies under stalks of flax on her roof. Rahab told the king's men, "Two men came here, but they left right before the city gate closed. If you leave now, there's still a chance you might catch them!"

The king's men rushed away, and Rahab went up on the roof to talk to the spies. She knew their God was very powerful because she had heard of the

things he had done for the Israelites in the desert. She told the spies, "We people of Jericho are afraid of you, because we know that the Lord has given you our land."

Rahab promised to help the spies escape if they would keep her entire family safe during the attack on Jericho. The men promised her that they would be kind to her and her family when the Israelites took over the city. Rahab lowered the spies down out of a window with a rope. She whispered to them, "Run and hide so they won't find you!"

The spies told her, "Gather your whole family in this house and stay here. Hang this red cord out of the window. The cord will let our army know not to hurt you when we return to take the city."

The spies returned safely to Joshua and told him, "We are sure that the Lord will give us this land."

34

The Walls of Jericho

Joshua 1:9; 6:1-23

The first thing the Israelites had to do when they entered the Promised Land was to take over the city of Jericho. God promised Joshua, "Be strong and brave. Do not be afraid or worried, because I am with you wherever you go."

Jericho was a difficult city to conquer because it had very high walls all the way around. There was no way for the Israelites to get in. But God had a plan. He told Joshua, "March around the walls once a day for six days. None of the men should speak or make any noise. Only the priests should blow their horns. On the seventh day, march around the city seven times. When the priests give one long, loud blast on their horns, ask the men to shout as loudly as they can. Then the walls of Jericho will fall down, and the men can go into the city."

Joshua gathered his army and told them about God's plan. When the right time came, they did as the

Lord had told them. The first day, they marched around the city and then returned to their camp. The second day, they did the same. This went on until the sixth day. On the seventh day, they got up at dawn and marched around Jericho. But this time, instead of circling the city just once, they did it seven times. After marching around Jericho seven times, the priests gave a long, loud blast on their horns.

When the men heard the signal, they shouted with all their might, and the walls of Jericho crumbled and came tumbling down. Joshua did not forget the promise the two spies had made to Rahab. Joshua asked the spies to go into the city and rescue Rahab and her entire family.

35

Gideon

Joshua 24:29-31; Judges 6:1-23, 36-40

A long time after the battle of Jericho, Joshua died. He was an old man who had helped the Israelites obey God for many years.

After Joshua's death, sometimes the Israelites would follow God's rules very well, but other times they would stop obeying God and worship idols instead. This made God angry, and he would let the Israelites' enemies make life difficult for them. Then the people would cry to God for help, and God would forgive them and save them from their enemies. God chose different people called judges to lead the Israelites. One of the judges was named Gideon.

One day, Gideon was working when he looked up and saw the angel of the Lord. "The

Lord is with you, mighty hero!" the angel said.

"How can the Lord be with us when all these bad things are happening? God is letting the Midianites hurt us," Gideon replied.

"I am sending you to save Israel from the Midianites!" the Lord said.

"I can't," Gideon said. "I am the weakest person from the weakest family in my tribe."

"I will be with you," the Lord said. "You will win against the Midianites."

Gideon said to the Lord, "If you are really going to help me, show me a sign. Please wait while I bring you an offering." The angel of the Lord agreed, and Gideon brought him some food.

The angel of the Lord said, "See that rock over there? Put the food on it."

Gideon did what he said, and the angel of the Lord touched the food with his staff. Fire burst up from the rock and burned up the meat and bread. The angel of the Lord disappeared. Gideon was very frightened when he realized that he had really seen the angel of the Lord, but God told him not to be afraid.

Not long after, several armies joined forces against Israel. Gideon knew it was time for him to help his people, but he was still a bit nervous. He said to God, "I'll put a fleece on the ground tonight. In the morning, if it is wet with dew and the ground is dry, I will know I am going to save the Israelites."

The next morning, God made the fleece wet and the ground dry, but Gideon wanted even more proof. "I want to be really sure, God," he said. "This time, can you make the fleece dry and the ground around it wet?"

God did what Gideon asked. Finally, Gideon was convinced that God would be with him and would help him save the Israelites.

36

Gideon's 300 Soldiers

Judges 6:34-35; 7:1-25

Gideon called for the men of Israel to form an
army to fight the Midianites. When everyone had
come, Gideon counted 32 thousand soldiers. God said
to Gideon, "You have too many soldiers in your army.
If you win against the Midianites, you will think that
you were strong enough to save yourselves. Tell the
soldiers that if any of them are scared, they can go
home." Gideon did as God said, and 22 thousand men
went home while 10 thousand men stayed.

"There are still too many," the Lord said.
"Take them to the stream to get a drink of
water, and I will tell you who will go with you
and who will not." When Gideon took the
men to the stream, God told him, "Watch
how the men drink water from the stream.
Put the men who use their hands like a
cup in one group, and in the other
group put the men who kneel
down and put their faces right
into the water." So Gideon
did. Only 300 men drank

111

water from their hands. "Those men will be in your army," God said. "Tell everyone else to go home."

Gideon and his 300 soldiers hid in the mountains above the Midianites' camp. Gideon divided the 300 men into three groups and handed each man a trumpet and a clay jar with a torch in it. He said, "Watch me closely. When I reach the edge of the camp, do as I do! When you see me blow the trumpet, it will be a sign for you to blow your trumpet too. Then shout, 'For the Lord and for Gideon!'"

Gideon's men followed his directions. In the middle of the night, while most of the Midianites were sleeping, Gideon and his army blew their trumpets, broke their clay jars, and shouted as loud as they could. The Midianites were terrified by the noise. God confused the Midianites, and they started to fight against and kill one another. Those who weren't killed ran as far away as they could. God had kept his promise to be with Gideon and save his people!

37

Samson

Judges 13:1–16:31

The Israelites kept disobeying God, so God kept letting their enemies rule over them. Then the people would be sorry for their sins and ask God for help, and God would send them another judge to help them.

Many years after Gideon defeated the Midianites, a group of people called the Philistines were ruling over the Israelites. There was an Israelite man named Manoah who didn't have any children. One day, the angel of the Lord appeared to Manoah's wife and told her that she would soon have a baby boy. The angel told Manoah and his wife that God had special plans

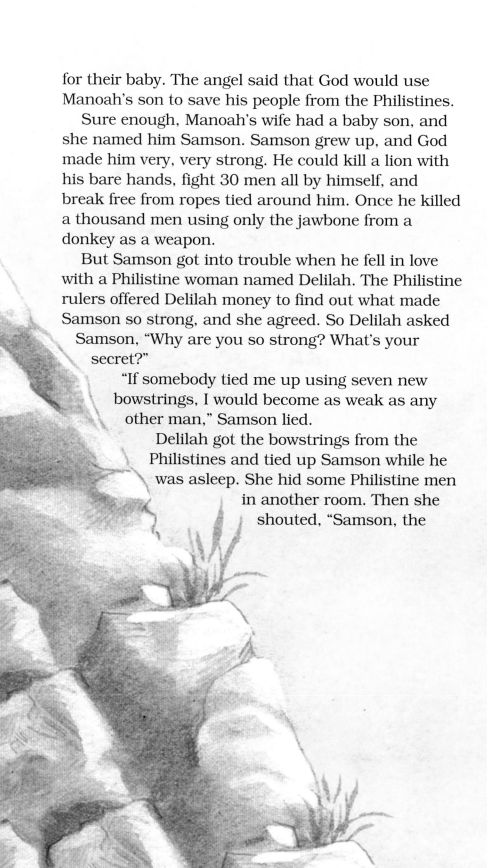

for their baby. The angel said that God would use Manoah's son to save his people from the Philistines.

Sure enough, Manoah's wife had a baby son, and she named him Samson. Samson grew up, and God made him very, very strong. He could kill a lion with his bare hands, fight 30 men all by himself, and break free from ropes tied around him. Once he killed a thousand men using only the jawbone from a donkey as a weapon.

But Samson got into trouble when he fell in love with a Philistine woman named Delilah. The Philistine rulers offered Delilah money to find out what made Samson so strong, and she agreed. So Delilah asked Samson, "Why are you so strong? What's your secret?"

"If somebody tied me up using seven new bowstrings, I would become as weak as any other man," Samson lied.

Delilah got the bowstrings from the Philistines and tied up Samson while he was asleep. She hid some Philistine men in another room. Then she shouted, "Samson, the

Philistines are here to capture you!" The Philistines rushed in and tried to capture Samson, but he easily broke free from the bowstrings.

Day after day, Delilah asked Samson to tell her the secret of his strength, but he kept lying to her. "Samson, if you really loved me you would tell me the truth," Delilah cried. She kept crying and asking Samson over and over until he couldn't stand it anymore.

Finally Samson said, "Before I was born, God told my parents never to cut my hair. If it were ever cut, I'd lose my strength."

Samson fell asleep with his head in Delilah's lap, and she called for a man to come and cut Samson's hair. Samson's strength left him, and the Philistines were able to capture him. They chained him up in a prison and made him grind their grain. But soon, Samson's hair began to grow again.

One day the Philistines were having a big party to worship one of their false gods, and they brought Samson out of prison so they could laugh at him. Samson stood between two of the pillars that were holding up the temple roof. Samson prayed, "God, please give me my strength back one more time." Samson pushed the two pillars with all his might, and the roof of the temple came crashing down on all the Philistines and on Samson, too. In his death, Samson killed more Philistines than he had when he was alive.

38

Naomi and Ruth

Ruth 1:1–4:22

Many years later, there was a famine in Israel, and people didn't have enough to eat. So a man named Elimelech left Israel and moved to a country called Moab with his wife, Naomi, and their two sons. They lived in Moab for a long time, and then Elimelech died.

Naomi's two sons, Mahlon and Kilion, grew up and married two Moabite women, Ruth and Orpah. Some time later Mahlon and Kilion also died, leaving both Naomi and her two daughters-in-law as widows. When Naomi heard that God had provided food for his people in Israel, she thought it was time to return to her home country. Orpah, Ruth, and Naomi packed up all their belongings and started the trip to Israel, but on the way, Naomi thought it would be better for Orpah and Ruth to go back to their parents' homes instead of going with her. Orpah went back to Moab, but Ruth wanted to stay with Naomi.

In Bethlehem, Ruth told Naomi, "I will go to the fields where I will pick up leftover grain so we can have food to eat."

Ruth ended up working in the fields of a man named Boaz, who was one of Naomi's relatives. Boaz noticed Ruth in the fields and told her, "I know how kind you have been to your mother-in-law. You left your parents and your homeland to go with her to live among strangers. May God bless you for it." Boaz then told Ruth that she should stay in his fields and pick up as much grain as she needed.

Ruth worked hard in the field that day. When Ruth got home, Naomi was surprised to see how much food she had been able to gather. When Ruth told Naomi about Boaz, Naomi told her to keep working in Boaz's fields.

One day, Naomi said to Ruth, "You should get married again, and Boaz is a good man. Put on your best clothes and some perfume and go see him tonight." Ruth followed Naomi's advice, and Boaz agreed to marry Ruth. Soon God gave them a son. They named their son Obed, and Naomi loved him very much.

39

The Boy Who Listened to God

1 Samuel 1:1-28; 3:1-21

Once there was an Israelite man named Elkanah who had two wives. One of his wives, Hannah, was very sad because Elkanah's other wife, Peninnah, had children, but Hannah did not have any. Peninnah would often make fun of Hannah because she couldn't have children. Elkanah took his family to the Tabernacle every year to worship God. At the Tabernacle, Hannah prayed to God for a son. She promised God, "If you give me a son, I will give him back to you so he can serve you."

The priest, Eli, saw Hannah praying. He told her, "May God answer your prayer."

God did answer Hannah's prayer, and soon she had a baby boy. She named him Samuel, which means "heard by God."

A few years later, Hannah took Samuel to the Tabernacle to keep her promise to God. Samuel lived in the Tabernacle and helped Eli, the priest. One night after he had gone to bed, Samuel heard somebody call out his name: "Samuel, Samuel." He got up and ran to Eli. "What is it?" Samuel asked. "Did you call me?"

Eli said, "I didn't call you. Go back to sleep." So Samuel went back to bed.

The Lord called Samuel a second time, but Samuel thought it was Eli again. "Here I am," he told the priest.

Eli answered, "No, I didn't call you." And so Samuel went back to bed again.

God called Samuel's name a third time, and once again Samuel ran to Eli. Eli realized that it must be God who was calling Samuel. "Samuel, go back to bed," he said. "If you hear your name being called again, say, 'Yes, Lord, I am here, listening to you.'"

When the Lord called out his name again, Samuel replied, "Yes, Lord, your servant is listening."

God told Samuel about the punishment he would give Eli's family, because Eli's sons were doing terrible things and Eli wasn't stopping them.

The next day, Eli asked Samuel what the Lord had said, and Samuel told him everything. After hearing the bad news, Eli said, "He is God. Let him do what he thinks is best."

Samuel grew up, and the people of Israel recognized that he was God's prophet who always listened to God and told the truth.

40
King Saul

1 Samuel 8:1–10:27; 15:1-35

Samuel was Israel's last judge. He had two sons, but they did not obey God like Samuel did. When Samuel was old, the leaders of Israel told him that since his sons could not be trusted, they would rather have a king instead of a judge. This made Samuel upset, but the Lord said, "The people are going against me, Samuel, not you. They don't want me to be their king anymore. Give them a king like they asked for, but tell them that bad things will happen

because of this." Samuel told the people that a king would make things worse for Israel, but the people did not listen.

God helped Samuel find Israel's new king. He chose a tall, handsome young man named Saul. Saul's father had sent him to look for their missing donkeys, but they were nowhere to be found. So Saul and his servant went to Samuel to ask for his help. But when Samuel saw Saul, the Lord told him that Saul was the man he had chosen to be the king.

King Saul led the people into battle and won against Israel's enemies. The people were happy with their new king, and God reminded Saul to obey him all the time.

When the Israelite army was about to fight against their enemies the Amalekites, God told Saul to destroy everything that belonged to them. But King Saul did not obey God's instructions. Saul attacked the Amalekites, but he kept the best of what they had for himself. God said, "I am sorry that I ever made Saul king, because he is not following me or doing what I tell him to."

King Saul tried to make excuses, but Samuel scolded him, saying, "Because you disobeyed God's instructions, God will choose a new king for Israel."

41

A Shepherd Boy
Becomes King

1 Samuel 16:1-13

One day, the Lord told Samuel, "Go to Bethlehem. There you will find a man named Jesse. I have chosen one of his sons to be Israel's new king. I will show you which one."

When Samuel arrived at Bethlehem, he invited Jesse and his sons to worship God with him. When Samuel met Jesse's oldest son, Eliab, he thought, "I'm sure this young man is God's choice!"

But God said to Samuel, "Don't choose the one that is the tallest or handsomest. I look at what is in the heart. Eliab is not the one." Jesse asked his son Abinadab to walk in front of Samuel, but the Lord said, "Not this one either." Samuel said, "Next," and Shammah passed by, but again the Lord said, "No, he is not the one either." This happened seven times as Jesse introduced his sons to Samuel. None of them were God's chosen king. "Are these all your sons?" Samuel asked Jesse.

"The youngest one is in the fields, watching the sheep," Jesse replied.

"Ask him to come," Samuel said. "We will wait until he gets here."

When Jesse's youngest son, David, came, the Lord said to Samuel, "This is the one. He will be Israel's next king."

Samuel took the olive oil he brought with him and poured it over David's head to show that God had chosen him. And God's powerful Spirit was with David from that moment on.

42
David and Goliath

1 Samuel 17:1-52

The Israelites' enemies the Philistines had decided to attack Israel again. Goliath, the Philistines' greatest warrior, shouted, "Who wants to fight me?" to the Israelite soldiers. Goliath was nine feet tall and very strong. He wore lots of armor and carried huge weapons. "Choose somebody from your army. If he is able to beat me, all of us Philistines will become your slaves. But if I beat him, then you will all be our slaves," Goliath yelled.

Nobody in King Saul's army was willing to fight the giant. One day, David brought food to his three brothers who were soldiers. He saw Goliath and heard what he was saying to the Israelites.

David told
the king, "I will
fight this Philistine
who is making fun of Israel."
King Saul said to David, "You
can't fight him! You are just a child, and
Goliath has been a soldier since he was a boy!"
But David said, "As a shepherd, I have protected
my father's sheep from bears and lions. God helped
me when I fought them. He will help me fight this
Philistine."

"All right," King Saul said. "Go, and may the Lord
be with you." He gave David his own armor and
sword, but they were too big. David took them off and
instead went to a nearby stream and picked up five
smooth stones. With only his staff, his sling, and his
bag with stones, David marched toward Goliath.

When Goliath saw a young boy coming to fight
him, he laughed. "What do you think you're going to
do to me with that little stick?" he shouted.

David said, "You come to me with your sword and
spear, but I come to you in the name of the one true
God. When I defeat you, the world will know that
Israel's God is the real God!"

As Goliath walked toward him, David reached into
his bag and took out a stone. Swinging the sling with
all his might, he threw the stone, and it hit Goliath in
his forehead. Goliath crashed to the ground. David
picked up Goliath's sword, and he killed the giant
with it. When the Philistines saw that their strongest
soldier was dead, they ran away.

Goliath might have been big and strong, but his
strength was nothing compared to God's.

43

Saul and David

1 Samuel 18:1-6; 19:9-10; 24:1-22

After David killed Goliath, King Saul asked David to be one of his helpers. Eventually Saul put David in charge of Israel's army. The people loved David, and he became a hero all over the country. This made King Saul jealous.

One time when King Saul was in a bad mood, he asked David to play the harp for him. While David was playing, Saul suddenly hurled his spear at David but missed him. David continued to do everything well, and Saul got more and more jealous of him.

Soon King Saul hated David so much that David had to run away. He went into the desert and stayed in caves. Some of his soldiers went with him. Saul and his other soldiers chased after David. One day David and his men were hiding far back in a cave, when Saul came in! Saul didn't see them. David's men whispered to David, "Now's your chance! Kill him!" David quietly moved closer to the king. He took his knife and cut off a piece of cloth from the bottom of King Saul's robe.

After King Saul left the cave, David called out to him, "My king! Don't listen to the people who say that

I am trying to kill you. I was inside that cave with you. Some of my men told me to kill you, but I told them that I will never harm you because you are God's chosen king. Look at what I have in my hand. This is a piece of your robe! I was close enough that I could have killed you, but I didn't."

King Saul cried and said to David, "You are a better man than I am, because you have repaid the bad things I have done to you with good. May God reward you for your kindness. You are surely going to be king." King Saul was right. Some years later, King Saul died in battle, and David became king of Israel.

44

Wise King Solomon

1 Kings 3:1-28

King David had a son named Solomon. After King David died, Solomon became the king of Israel. One night God appeared to him in a dream and told him, "Solomon, ask for whatever you want me to give you."

Solomon answered, "Please give me wisdom so I can lead your people well."

God was happy with Solomon's reply. He said, "Because you have asked for wisdom instead of a long life, money, or the death of your enemies, I will give you what you asked for. You will have more wisdom and understanding than anyone has ever had. I will also give you wealth and fame, even though you didn't ask for it. I will give you a long life if you honor and obey me like your father, David, did."

King Solomon soon got a chance to use the wisdom God gave him. Two women came to the king to settle an argument. One of the women said, "This woman and I live together in one house. We both had babies only three days apart. But her baby died one night while she was sleeping. In the middle of the night, she took my son away from me and swapped her dead son for mine."

"That's not true," said the other woman. "The living baby is mine and the dead one is yours." The women argued back and forth in front of the king.

Finally, King Solomon asked for a sword. "Cut the living baby in two and give both of these women a half each," he ordered.

The real mother of the living baby cried out, "No, no, please don't! Give her the baby. Just don't kill him!"

The other woman said, "Neither one of us will have this baby. Divide him between us!"

King Solomon said, "The woman who wants him to live loves him. She is his real mother. Give the baby to her!" Everyone was amazed at the king's wise solution to the problem.

45

Elijah

1 Kings 17:1-16; 18:1-2, 16-39

After King Solomon died, the kingdom of Israel was split into two—the northern kingdom, Israel, and the southern kingdom, Judah. Many kings ruled the two kingdoms. Most of them did not follow God, and they led the people into worshiping idols. King Ahab was one of the northern kingdom's most evil rulers.

Elijah was a prophet, someone who listened to God and spoke his messages to the people. God told Elijah to tell Ahab, "I am not pleased with you, and there will be no more rain for the next few years."

This was very bad news for Ahab, because without rain to help the crops grow,

143

there would be no food. Ahab got so angry at Elijah that the prophet had to run away and hide. God took care of Elijah and sent ravens to carry food to him. He drank water from a brook nearby. When the brook dried up, God showed him a village where a widow let him stay in her house. God did a miracle so that there was always enough food in the house for the widow, her son, and Elijah.

There had been no rain for almost three years when God asked Elijah to go see King Ahab again. The king was furious. "There you are, you troublemaker!" he said to Elijah.

Elijah replied, "You are the one who has made trouble for Israel by worshiping the false god Baal. Let's have a contest to see whose God is the true God! Gather the people of Israel and the 450 prophets of Baal at Mount Carmel."

Ahab agreed, and all the people went up to Mount Carmel to watch Elijah's contest against the prophets of Baal. Elijah built an altar and put a sacrifice on it, and Baal's prophets did the same. "Now," Elijah said, "ask your god to send fire to burn up the sacrifice. The God who sends fire is the true God!"

The prophets of Baal went first. They shouted, danced, and even hurt themselves to try to get Baal's attention. But nothing happened.

Then it was Elijah's turn. He asked some people to pour huge jars of water over his altar, so that if it caught fire, everyone would know it was not by chance. Then Elijah prayed, "O Lord, prove to us today that you are the true God!" Immediately fire came down from heaven and burned up the sacrifice and the entire altar, stones and all. The people fell on their faces on the ground and cried out, "The Lord is God!"

46

Elijah Is Taken Up to Heaven

1 Kings 19:19-21; 2 Kings 2:1-15

Elijah was getting old, and God told him to ask a man named Elisha to be his helper. God wanted Elisha to help Elijah and later take his place as God's prophet.

One day as Elijah and Elisha were traveling from a town called Gilgal, Elijah said to Elisha, "Stay here! The Lord wants me to go to Bethel."

But Elisha said, "I will never leave your side." So they went to Bethel together.

When they arrived in Bethel, a group of prophets came up to Elisha and said, "Did you know that God will take your master away from you today?"

"Yes, I know," Elisha replied, "but I don't want to talk about it."

Then Elijah told Elisha, "Stay here! The Lord wants me to go to Jericho." But Elisha gave the same answer as the first time. When they arrived in Jericho, again a group of prophets

came up to Elisha. They said the same thing as the prophets in Bethel had, and Elisha gave them the same answer.

Once again Elijah said to Elisha, "Stay here! The Lord wants me to go to the Jordan River." One more time, Elisha said, "I will never leave you." So they went together.

When they got to the Jordan River, Elijah took off his coat, rolled it up, and hit the water with it. The water split, piling up on the right and the left, and Elijah and Elisha were able to cross the river walking on dry ground.

When they were on the other side, Elijah asked Elisha, "What do you want me to do for you before I am taken away?"

Elisha replied, "Please let me get a double share of the spirit you have."

"That's a difficult request," Elijah said. "If you see me when I am taken away, you will get it. Otherwise you won't." As they were talking, a chariot made of fire and pulled by fiery horses appeared. The chariot drove between them, and Elijah was taken up to heaven in a whirlwind. As he left, Elijah's coat fell to the ground. Elisha saw everything and cried out, "My father! My father! I see the chariots and charioteers of Israel!" Then Elijah and the chariot of fire disappeared.

Elisha picked up Elijah's coat, went to the bank of the Jordan River, and hit the water with the coat. "Where is the God of Elijah?" he said. The river water split just as it had done before, and Elisha crossed on dry ground. Then the people watching knew that the same spirit that had been in Elijah was now in Elisha.

47

Elisha

2 Kings 2:19-22; 3:1-25; 4:1-37

God gave Elisha the power to do great and mighty
things. One day some rulers from Jericho came to
ask Elisha to help them with the city's water problem.
Their water was not good for drinking or for growing
crops. Elisha asked for a bowl filled with salt. He
threw the salt into the spring that Jericho's water
came from. "This water has now been healed by the
Lord," he said.

Elisha performed many other miracles. He helped
three kings when they ran out of water while their
armies were on their way to battle the Moabites, who
were enemies of Israel. Not only did Elisha tell them
that God would provide water for them, he also said
that they would win over their enemy. And everything
happened just as he said.

Another time, a widow came to Elisha asking
for help. Her two children were about to be
taken as slaves because her dead husband
had owed money she couldn't pay back.
Elisha asked the widow to get all the jugs
she could find. Elisha told her, "You have

151

a little bit of oil in your house. Pour the oil into each jug until they are all full." The woman poured and poured, but the oil didn't run out until she had filled all the jugs. Elisha told her, "Go and sell the oil so you can repay the money your husband owed."

Whenever Elisha traveled to the town of Shunem, he always stayed with a certain woman and her husband. The woman even set up a special room for Elisha in their house. The woman and her husband had no children, but one day Elisha told the woman, "One year from now, you will have a son in your arms." Elisha's words came true. The woman got pregnant and had a baby boy.

Several years later, the boy was with his father in the field. He began to complain, "My head hurts so much!" The boy's father told a servant to carry his son back home to his mother. She held her son in her lap, but the boy died shortly after. The boy's mother laid him on the bed that Elisha used and went to find Elisha. Elisha went to her house and found the boy lying on his bed. Elisha got on the bed with the boy and prayed. God heard Elisha's prayer and brought the boy back to life. The boy's mother was so happy to see her son alive again!

48

Naaman Is Healed

2 Kings 5:1-27

Naaman was a great soldier, the leader of the entire army of the country of Aram. The king of Aram liked Naaman very much because he won so many battles. But Naaman had leprosy, a horrible skin disease. No one knew how to cure it, and Naaman kept getting worse and worse.

The Arameans had fought against the Israelites and had taken some Israelite people as prisoners. One of these people was a young girl who had become a maid for Naaman's wife. One day the girl said to her mistress, "I wish my master would go see the prophet Elisha in Israel. Elisha could cure his leprosy!" So Naaman went to see Elisha.

Naaman took a group of helpers with him and went to Elisha's house. Elisha sent a messenger to meet Naaman at the door and tell him to go wash in the Jordan River seven times and he would be healed. This made Naaman angry. "Why won't Elisha even come out to talk to me? Besides, aren't the rivers in Aram better than all the rivers in Israel?" Naaman was ready to leave, but his helpers convinced him to follow Elisha's instructions.

So Naaman went to the Jordan River and dunked himself in the water seven times, as Elisha had told him to. When he came out of the water the seventh time, his leprosy was gone! Naaman and his helpers went back to Elisha's house to thank the prophet.

"There is no other God except the God of Israel," Naaman told Elisha. "Please, let me give you a gift to say thank you." But Elisha wouldn't take any gifts.

Naaman was heading back home when he was stopped by Elisha's servant Gehazi. When Naaman asked Gehazi what he needed, Elisha's servant lied and said, "My master sent me to tell you that two young prophets have just arrived. He would like to have 75 pounds of silver and two sets of clothes for them."

Naaman happily gave Gehazi the two sets of clothes and twice as much silver as he had asked for. He even asked two of his servants to help Gehazi carry the gifts back with him. When they arrived at the hill where Elisha lived, Gehazi took the gifts and stored them in his house. When he went to see Elisha, his master asked him, "Where have you been, Gehazi?"

"Nowhere," Gehazi said.

Elisha said, "I was with you in spirit when you talked to Naaman. Is this the time to be greedy? From now on, you and your family will have Naaman's leprosy. But for you, there will be no cure." As soon as Gehazi left the room his skin was covered with leprosy.

49

The Story of Esther

Esther 1:1–8:17; 9:20-32

Over the years, God sent many prophets to tell his people how to obey him and to warn them of what would happen if they disobeyed. But the Israelites did not listen. Finally God allowed some of Israel's enemies to take over the land and to take the people as prisoners. Some of the Israelites ended up in the kingdom of Persia.

One day the king of Persia, Xerxes, decided that he didn't want to be married to his wife, Queen Vashti, anymore, so he sent her away. After a while, King Xerxes decided that he wanted a new queen. His helpers suggested that he bring all the beautiful young women in the kingdom into his palace so he could choose which one he liked best. The king thought this was a good idea, so that's what happened.

One of the beautiful girls who came to the palace was named Esther. Esther was an Israelite. Both of her parents had died, and her cousin Mordecai had taken care of her since she was young. Mordecai worked in King Xerxes's palace. When Esther was taken to the palace, Mordecai told her not to tell anyone that she was an Israelite.

Esther did as Mordecai said. Soon King Xerxes decided that Esther was his favorite out of all of the young women, and he made her his new queen. Meanwhile, Mordecai got in trouble with a man named Haman, who was the king's most important helper. Haman wanted everyone to bow down in front of him when he went by. But Mordecai would not bow down in front of Haman. This made Haman furious. Since he knew that Mordecai was an Israelite, he asked the king to sign a law saying that all Israelites should be killed.

When he learned about the new law, Mordecai asked Esther for help. "Go to the king and ask him to change the law," he said. "Maybe this is the reason why you've become the queen—so that you can save our people."

At first Esther was afraid, because no one was supposed

to go see the king without permission. The king could punish or even kill Esther for disobeying him. But Esther knew she needed to be brave and help her people. So she asked Mordecai to pray for her, and then she went to see the king.

The king wasn't angry when he saw Esther—in fact, he was happy to see her! "What do you want, Queen Esther?" he asked. "Whatever you ask, I will give it to you." Esther had a plan. She invited the king and Haman to a party. Both men were glad to come.

At the party, the king once again asked Esther, "What can I do for you? I will give you what you ask, even if it is half of my kingdom."

Esther replied, "Please come with Haman to another party I will give for you tomorrow. Then I will tell you what I need."

Meanwhile Haman continued making evil plans. He was getting ready to ask the king to kill Mordecai.

The next day, at Esther's second party, the king asked Esther what she wanted yet again. The queen finally said, "Please save my life and the lives of my people!"

The king couldn't believe it. "Who would dare hurt you?" he asked.

"Haman is the one who wants to kill me and all my people," Queen Esther told the king. The king was furious. He ordered that Haman be killed in the same way that Haman had planned to kill Mordecai. Then the king made a new law that said that the Israelites could defend themselves from anyone who tried to hurt them. The king made Mordecai one of his most important helpers. Every year after that, the Israelites celebrated a holiday to remember how Queen Esther had saved her people.

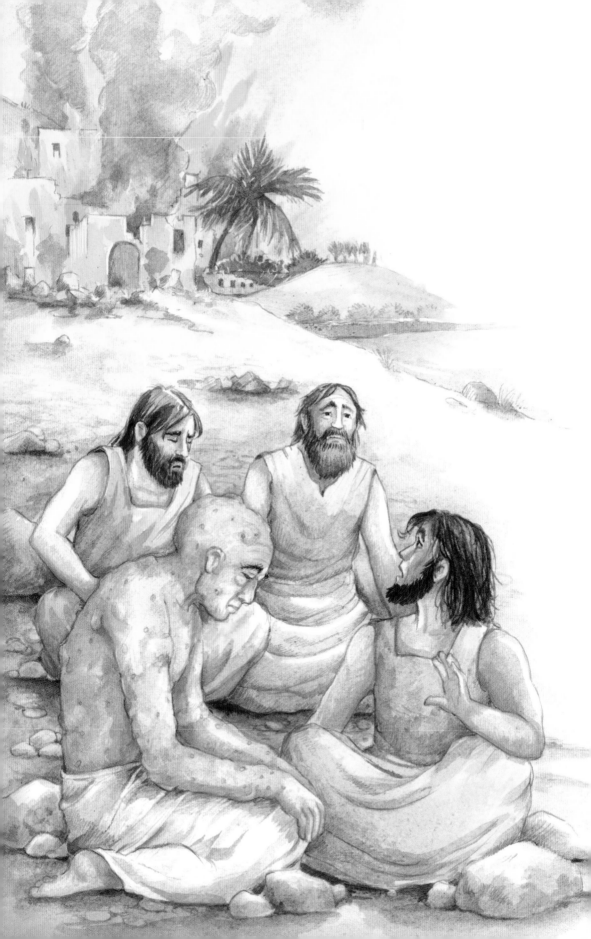

50

The Story of Job

Job 1:1–2:13; 42:7-16

There once lived a man named Job who obeyed God and always tried to do the right thing. He had lots of riches and a big family. He owned thousands of animals. God was very pleased with Job because of how he followed God.

One day, Satan, God's enemy, came and stood before God. Satan said that Job only obeyed God because life was easy for him. "Look at all the wonderful things you've given Job!" Satan said. "If you take them away, he will hate you."

"All right," God told Satan. "I will allow you to take everything away from Job, but don't harm him."

In one terrible day, Job lost all of his animals, almost all of his servants, and all his children. Job's heart was broken. But he did not turn away from God. He said, "I had nothing when I was born, and I will have nothing when I die. The Lord gives, and the Lord takes away. I will praise his name!"

Satan came back and stood before God again. "Have you seen my servant Job?" God said. "You took away everything he had, but he still follows me."

"No one cares about anything more than his own body," Satan replied. "If you let me take away his health, he will hate you."

"All right," God said. "You may make him sick, but don't kill him."

So Satan gave Job painful sores from head to toe. Job's wife asked him, "Are you still trusting God? Curse him so that you can die."

"No," Job said. "That is a foolish way to talk. Should we only take the good things God gives us and not the bad?" In all that Job said and did he stayed faithful to God.

God was pleased that even through Job's pain and hardships, Job continued to trust him. God gave Job twice as many animals and blessed him with seven more sons and three more daughters. And Job kept following God faithfully all the days of his life.

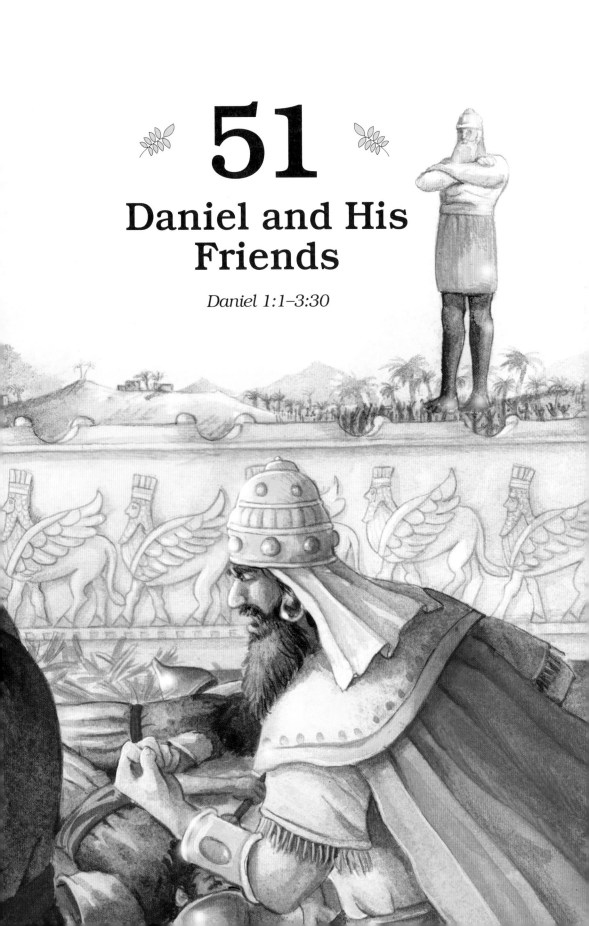

51

Daniel and His Friends

Daniel 1:1–3:30

One of the enemies that God used to punish the southern kingdom of Judah was King Nebuchadnezzar of Babylon. King Nebuchadnezzar destroyed Judah's capital city, Jerusalem, and took many of the people of Judah as prisoners. Four of the prisoners were young men named Daniel, Shadrach, Meshach, and Abednego. They were brought to Babylon and trained to serve King Nebuchadnezzar. After their training, the king was very pleased with the four young men and made them his helpers. Later, the king had an upsetting dream, and Daniel was able to tell him what it meant. King Nebuchadnezzar made Daniel one of his most important helpers, and Daniel asked that Shadrach, Meshach, and Abednego be given important jobs as well.

Then one day King Nebuchadnezzar decided to make a huge golden statue. He ordered all of his assistants to come worship the statue. The king's messenger said, "The king commands that when the music starts to play, everyone should bow down to worship King Nebuchadnezzar's statue. Anyone who does not worship it will be thrown into a flaming furnace and burned to death." Shadrach, Meshach, and Abednego were there with the king's other helpers.

As soon as the music began, all the king's helpers fell to the ground to worship the statue—all except

three. Shadrach, Meshach, and Abednego did not bow down to the statue. The king ordered them to stand before him and gave them one more chance to worship the statue. But the three friends said, "If we are thrown into the flaming furnace, our God will protect us. But even if he doesn't, we still will not serve your gods or worship your statue."

This made King Nebuchadnezzar furious. "Make the furnace seven times hotter!" he ordered. The furnace got so hot that the flames killed the soldiers who threw the three friends inside it. Then the king noticed something strange. There were four men inside the furnace instead of three. They were walking around in the fire, not burned or hurt at all. "That fourth man looks like a god!" the king exclaimed. He shouted, "Shadrach, Meshach, and Abednego, come out."

When Shadrach, Meshach, and Abednego stepped out of the furnace, they were completely unharmed. They didn't even smell like smoke. They had trusted God, and he had saved them from the fire.

The king said, "Praise your God, who has sent an angel to protect you. There is no other god like him!"

❧ **52** ❧

Daniel and the Lions

Daniel 6:1-28

Daniel served King Nebuchadnezzar and then the kings who came after him. After the Persians conquered the Babylonians, Daniel served the Persian king Darius. King Darius liked Daniel very much and wanted to make him leader over the entire empire. But not everyone was happy about this. The king's other helpers became jealous of Daniel. They thought and thought about what they could do to get him in trouble. But Daniel was an honest man who did his job well. It was impossible to find anything bad to say about him. "The only way we are going to get Daniel in trouble is if we can find a way to use his faith in God against him," they thought.

The helpers went to King Darius and asked him to make a new law. The law said that for 30 days, people should pray only to King Darius. Anybody who prayed to anyone else would be thrown into a den full of lions. Daniel heard about the new law, but it did not stop him from praying to God three times a day, just the same as he always had.

The king's jealous helpers went to Daniel's house and saw him praying. When they told the king about it, he was sad. But he could not change the law. With a sigh, the king ordered that Daniel be thrown into the lions' den. He said to Daniel, "May your God, the one you worship, save you."

The king headed back to the palace and went straight to bed. He didn't feel like eating or doing anything else. It was a long night, and he was not able to sleep at all. The next morning, the king rushed to the lions' den and called out, "Daniel, was your God able to save you from the lions?"

A voice came up from the lions' den! "Long live the king!" Daniel said. "My God sent his angel to shut the mouths of the lions so they couldn't hurt me, because I didn't do anything wrong against God or against you."

King Darius was so happy! He ordered that Daniel be taken out of the lions' den. The king then ordered that those who had accused Daniel be thrown into the lions' den instead.

King Darius told his people, "In every part of the kingdom, everyone should worship Daniel's God. He is the one true God. He protects his people and does great and mighty things, both in heaven and on earth. He rescued Daniel from the lions!"

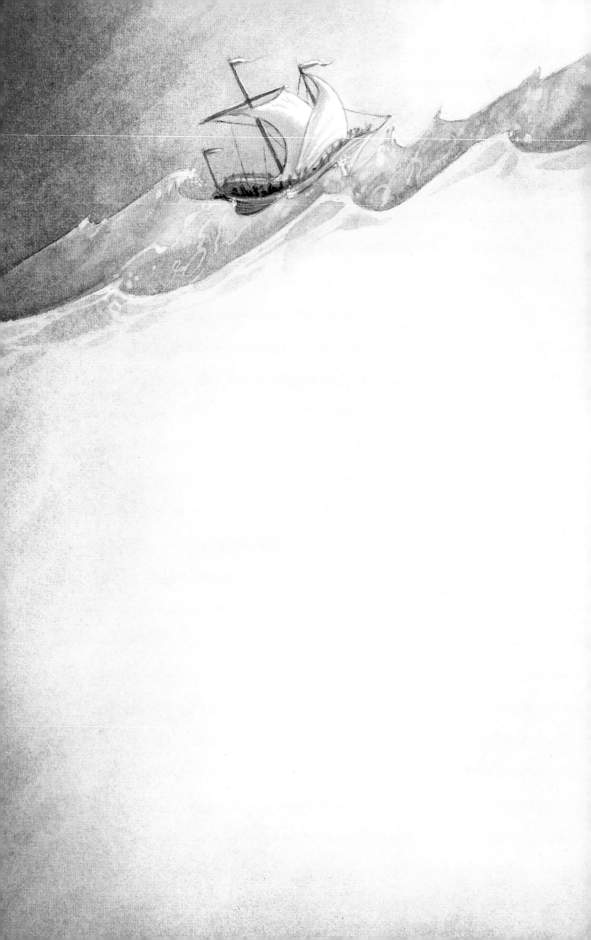

53

A Job for Jonah

Jonah 1:1–3:10

God had a job for Jonah, one of his prophets. He told Jonah, "Go to the city of Nineveh, and tell the people there that they have to stop doing bad things. Tell them that if they don't, I will destroy them!" But Jonah did not want to give God's message to the people of Nineveh. So he decided to run away. He got on a ship going the opposite direction from Nineveh.

While Jonah's ship was out at sea, God sent strong winds that made a huge storm. Jonah, sleeping below deck, was awakened by the frightened sailors. They were trying to find out who was responsible for the storm. Jonah confessed, "This storm is happening

because of me. If you want the storm to stop, throw me overboard!"

The sailors didn't want to throw Jonah in the water. They tried as hard as they could to row to shore, but the waves were too strong. So finally they prayed, "God, we will throw this man overboard, but please don't blame us for his death." And so they threw Jonah overboard, and immediately the storm stopped raging. Jonah started to sink to the bottom of the sea, but God sent a huge fish to swallow Jonah. For three days and three nights, Jonah lived in the belly of the fish.

From the belly of the fish Jonah cried out to God. He said he was sorry for not doing what God wanted him to do. He promised God, "I will do what you want me to do." God heard Jonah's prayers, and the fish spit out Jonah on the shore.

Jonah went to the city of Nineveh and gave the people God's message: "Nineveh will be destroyed in 40 days!"

The king of Nineveh listened to Jonah. He told his people, "None of us will eat or drink anything, to show God that we are sorry for all the evil things we have done. Maybe God will change his mind about punishing us."

The people of Nineveh did as he said. When God saw that they were sorry, he decided not to punish them.

New Testament

54

Gabriel Visits Mary

Luke 1:26-38

Many, many years after Jonah, a young woman named Mary was engaged to be married to a man named Joseph. One day Mary got a special visit from the angel Gabriel. He appeared to her and said, "Mary, you are truly blessed. The Lord is with you!"

Mary was surprised and confused, but the angel said to her, "Don't be afraid, Mary! God is pleased with you." Mary had no idea what the angel meant. Gabriel continued, "You will soon become pregnant and will have a baby boy. You will name him Jesus. He will be great and will be called the Son of God. He will reign over Israel, and his Kingdom will never end."

"How can this happen?" Mary asked. "I am not married, so how can I have a baby?"

Gabriel answered, "God's Holy Spirit will make it possible. The child will be holy, for he is the Son of God. God keeps every promise he makes."

Mary replied to the angel, "I am the Lord's servant. Let everything that you said come true!" Then the angel left.

55

Zechariah and Elizabeth

Luke 1:5-25

Zechariah was a priest in the Temple and followed God faithfully. He and his wife, Elizabeth, were both very old, and they had no children.

One day Zechariah was chosen to do a very special job in the Temple. While he was inside the Temple, the angel Gabriel suddenly appeared. Zechariah was startled and shook with fear. The angel told him, "Don't be afraid, Zechariah. The Lord has heard your prayer. Your wife, Elizabeth, will have a son, and you will name him John. Even before his birth, he will be filled with God's Holy Spirit. He will help many people turn to the Lord. He will prepare people's hearts for when the Messiah, the Savior sent from God, arrives."

Zechariah couldn't believe what he was hearing. He said to the angel, "This is impossible. I'm old, and so is my wife. We can't have children at our age."

Gabriel replied, "Because you didn't believe me, you won't be able to speak until your son is born. What I told you will come true."

When Zechariah came out of the Temple, he couldn't speak. His wife, Elizabeth, soon became pregnant. She said, "How kind God is for giving us this child!"

56

Jesus Is Born

Luke 2:1-7

In those days Israel had been conquered by the
Roman Empire. Caesar Augustus, the Roman emperor,
decided that everyone needed to go back to their
hometowns so he could count them and find out how
many people he ruled over. Joseph, Mary's fiancé, lived
in the town of Nazareth, but his family was from the
town of Bethlehem, so he had to go there. Mary made
the long journey with him, even though it was almost
time for her baby to be born.

Joseph and Mary finally reached Bethlehem, but
they had a problem. There was no place for them to
stay. Everywhere they looked was already full of
guests, because so many people had traveled to
Bethlehem to be counted. Finally someone offered
them a place to stay. It was a stable where animals
slept. That night Mary had her baby boy, and she
named him Jesus, like the angel had told her. Mary
wrapped baby Jesus in strips of cloth and laid him in
a manger, a box that usually held food for animals.
God's Son, the Savior of the world, was born.

57
Shepherds and Angels

Luke 2:8-20

In a nearby field, shepherds were watching over their flocks of sheep. All of a sudden an angel appeared, and God's glory shone brightly all around! The shepherds were terrified.

"Don't be afraid!" the angel told them. "I have good news for you that will bring great joy to everyone. Today the Savior has been born in Bethlehem. He is the baby you will find wrapped in strips of cloth, lying in a manger."

Suddenly more angels appeared, praising God: "Glory to God in highest heaven, and on earth let there be peace to those who please God."

When the angels had gone back to heaven, the shepherds said to each other, "Let's go to Bethlehem and see for ourselves what the angels have told us about." All of them went to Bethlehem, where they found Mary and Joseph and the baby lying in the

manger, just like the angel had said. The shepherds
worshiped Jesus, and their hearts were full of joy.
The shepherds couldn't keep the good news to

themselves. They told everyone they saw about what had happened. As for Mary, she kept all these things in her heart and continued to think about them.

58

The Wise Men Visit Jesus

Matthew 2:1-12

When Jesus was born, Herod was king of the Jews, ruling under the Roman emperor. Some wise men came from their home in the east to Jerusalem. They asked, "Where is the child who has been born to be king of the Jews? We have seen his star in the sky and have come to worship him."

King Herod was alarmed when he heard about the wise men and why they had come. He got all the high priests and scholars together and asked them, "Where will the Messiah be born?" They answered, "In Bethlehem."

Herod asked the wise men to tell him exactly when the star had first appeared. Herod told the wise men, "Go on your way. Do everything you can to find the new king. When you find him, tell me! I will join you in worshiping him." But Herod was lying. He wanted to kill the child who would be king.

The wise men went on their way. Looking up, they saw the same star they had seen in the east. The star guided them to Bethlehem. When they arrived at the house, the wise men saw Jesus with his mother, Mary. They knelt down and worshiped Jesus. They gave him beautiful gifts of gold, frankincense, and myrrh.

God had sent a dream to the wise men warning them not to go back to Herod. So when they left Jesus, they took another route back home.

59

Jesus in the Temple

Luke 2:41-52

Joseph and Mary went to celebrate the festival of
Passover in Jerusalem every year. When Jesus was
12 years old, he went with them. After the festival was
over, it was time to go back home. Joseph and Mary
didn't see Jesus during their first day of travel, but
they thought he was with another group of their
family and friends. But that night they couldn't find
him. Joseph and Mary had to go back to Jerusalem to
search for Jesus. After three days, they finally found
him. Jesus was in the Temple talking to teachers who
were much older than him. He was sitting with them,
listening and asking them questions. Everyone who
heard Jesus was impressed with his wisdom and
understanding. He didn't sound like an ordinary
12-year-old.

Mary asked Jesus, "Son, why did you do this to
us? We were so worried about you."

"Why were you searching?" Jesus replied. "Didn't
you know that I had to be in my Father's house?"

Jesus went home to Nazareth with his parents and
obeyed them. He grew wiser and stronger every day,
loved by God and people.

60

Jesus Begins His Work

Matthew 3:1–4:11

John, the son of Elizabeth and Zechariah, was all grown up and doing God's work. He was preaching God's message and telling people to repent of their sins. He baptized people in the Jordan River so they could show that they wanted to be cleaned from their sins and live a new life. That's why he was known as John the Baptist.

When Jesus was 30 years old, he came to the Jordan River and said to John, "I want you to baptize me."

John the Baptist protested, "I'm the one who needs to be baptized by you."

But Jesus said, "This is how it should be. We should do everything that God wants us to do." So John agreed to baptize Jesus.

When Jesus came up out of the water, the sky opened. The Spirit of God came down like a dove and landed on him. Then a voice from heaven said, "This is my dear Son, who brings me great joy."

Afterward the Holy Spirit guided Jesus into the wilderness. Jesus didn't eat anything for 40 days and 40 nights. Then God's enemy, Satan, came to tempt him to sin. Satan said, "If you are truly God's Son, you can turn these stones into loaves of bread."

Jesus answered, "God's Word says, 'People do not live on bread alone but by every word that comes from the mouth of God.'"

Then Satan led him to the roof of the Temple. He challenged Jesus, "If you are truly the Son of God, jump off! The Scriptures say that God will send his angels to save you from hitting the rocks below."

Jesus answered, "God's Word says, 'Do not test the Lord your God.'"

Then Satan took Jesus to the top of a high mountain. He said to Jesus, "Everything you see can be yours if you will only bow down and worship me."

Jesus answered, "God's Word says, 'Worship and serve only the Lord your God.'" Then Satan left Jesus, and angels came and helped him.

61

Follow Me

Mark 1:16-22, 29-39

Jesus was walking along the shore of the Sea of
Galilee when he saw a man named Simon and his
brother Andrew fishing. He called out to them, "Come,
follow me, and I will show you how to fish for people!"
Immediately Simon and Andrew left their nets and
joined Jesus. Going a little farther, Jesus saw another
set of brothers, James and John, who were in a boat
fixing their nets. Jesus called to them, too. James and
John left their father and followed Jesus. Jesus and
his new followers went to the town of Capernaum,
and on the morning of the Sabbath day, they went
to the synagogue, where Jesus preached. The people
there were amazed by the power of his words.

After leaving the synagogue, Jesus went to Simon's
home. When Jesus got there, people told him that

Simon's mother-in-law had a high fever. "Can you help her?" they asked. Jesus stood by her bedside, took her hand, and helped her up. Just like that, the sick woman's fever left. She felt so much better that she was able to get up and prepare a meal for Jesus and his friends. That evening, many people brought their sick relatives to Jesus. He touched them and healed them all.

Early the next morning, Jesus headed out to the desert to pray. When his friends found him, Simon told him, "Everyone is looking for you."

Jesus replied, "We must go to other towns. I must tell other people about the good news of the Kingdom of God." He traveled and preached in towns all around the region of Galilee.

62
Jesus Turns Water into Wine

John 2:1-11

One day there was a wedding in the town of Cana, and Jesus, his mother, and his disciples were invited. The celebration was going well until a big problem came up: the hosts ran out of wine. It would

be very embarrassing for the hosts if they did not have wine to serve to their guests. Mary found out about the problem and told Jesus about it.

"Dear woman, that's not our problem," Jesus told his mother. "It's not yet my time."

But Mary told the servants, "Whatever Jesus tells you to do, do it!"

Nearby Jesus saw six big stone jars. He asked the servants to fill the jars with water, all the way up to the brim. After all the jars were filled, Jesus said, "Dip some out and take it to the person in charge." The master of the banquet tasted it. He took a sip, and a big smile spread across his face. He called the groom over and told him, "People usually serve the best wine first and then serve the cheaper kind later. But you are different! You have saved the best wine until now!"

This first miracle of Jesus revealed his glory. And his disciples put their faith in him.

63

The Woman at the Well

John 4:1-42

Jesus and his disciples were heading to Galilee from Judea. To get there, Jesus wanted to pass through Samaria. This was surprising because the Samaritans and the Jews didn't like each other. Many Jews would rather take a longer route around Samaria so they didn't have to meet any Samaritans.

Jesus and his disciples stopped at a well in the Samaritan village of Sychar to rest. The disciples left Jesus there while they headed to the village to buy some food. After a little while, a Samaritan woman arrived to get water from the well. "Will you give me some water?" Jesus asked her.

"You're asking me?" the woman said, surprised. "Don't you know that Jews and Samaritans don't speak to each other?"

Jesus said, "If you knew who I was, you would ask me for some living water!"

The woman answered, "But the well is deep, and you don't even have a rope or a bucket. Where would you get this living water?"

Jesus answered, "Someone who drinks the water from this well will soon be thirsty again. But the people who drink the water I give will never be thirsty again. My water becomes a flowing fountain that gives eternal life."

The woman replied, "Please give me this water so that I will never be thirsty again."

Jesus said, "Go, call your husband and come back."

The woman said, "I don't have a husband."

Jesus told her, "That's very true. You have had five husbands, and you are not married to the man you're living with now."

The Samaritan woman was shocked that Jesus knew this about her. She said to him, "You must be a prophet. So tell me, why do you Jews say that Jerusalem is the only place to worship? My ancestors worshiped here at Mount Gerizim."

Jesus answered, "The time is coming when it won't matter whether we worship the Father here or in Jerusalem. God is looking for true worshipers."

The woman replied, "I know that the Messiah is coming. He will explain everything to us."

Jesus told her, "I am the Messiah!"

The woman ran back to town and told people about her meeting with Jesus. "Come and see a man who told me everything I ever did!" she said. "Could he be the Messiah?" The people rushed to see Jesus, and many of them put their faith in him.

64

The Storm Obeys Jesus

Mark 4:35-41; Luke 8:22-25

Jesus had been teaching people by the Sea of Galilee. One evening, Jesus said to his disciples, "Let's go to the other side of the lake." So they all got into a boat and set off across the lake. As they were sailing, Jesus fell asleep. Then a huge storm came up, and the wind and the waves rocked the boat hard, up and down. Water started to fill the boat, and the disciples started to panic. "What are we going to do? We're going to drown!"

The disciples found Jesus asleep in the back of the boat and woke him up. "Jesus! Jesus!" they shouted. "Don't you care that we might die?"

Jesus stood up and spoke to the wind and the sea. "Wind, stop blowing. Waves, be still!" Right away the wind stopped blowing, and the sea became calm. Jesus turned to his disciples and said, "Why are you afraid? Where is your faith?"

The disciples were terrified and amazed. They looked at each other and said, "Who is this man who can command even the wind and the sea?"

211

65

A Hole in the Roof

Mark 2:1-12; Luke 5:17-26

One day Jesus was teaching in the town of
Capernaum. People were excited to see him. They
crowded into the house where he was staying. Soon
the house was packed with so many visitors that there
was no space for even one more person to get in.

As everyone was listening to Jesus, suddenly they
heard a noise from the ceiling. Soon a hole opened up
in the ceiling. Four men carefully lowered their
paralyzed friend on a mat through the hole in the
roof. They hadn't been able to get him through the
door because of the crowd, so they found another way
to get their friend to Jesus. Jesus was happy to see
that they had so much faith. He said to the paralyzed
man, "Young man, your sins are forgiven."

There were some priests and Jewish teachers

there, and they did not like what they heard. "Who does Jesus think he is?" they thought to themselves. "Only God can forgive sins!"

Jesus knew what they were thinking. He said out loud for everyone to hear, "Why do you question me in your hearts? Which is easier, to say to this man, 'Your sins are forgiven,' or to say, 'Stand up and walk'? I will prove to you that I have the power to forgive sins."

Jesus turned to the paralyzed man and told him, "Get up, pick up your mat, and go home!" The paralyzed man did as Jesus said. He stood up, got his mat, and walked home, praising God. The people were amazed. "We have never seen anything like this before!" they said.

66

The Beatitudes

Matthew 5:1-12

One day, Jesus went up on a mountainside and sat down. His disciples came and sat near him, and he began to teach them about how God wants people to live.

"God blesses people who realize that they need him," Jesus said. "The Kingdom of Heaven will belong to them.

"God blesses people who are sad. He will comfort them.

"God blesses people who are humble. He will give them the whole earth.

"God blesses people who always want to do what is right. God will make sure that they are satisfied.

"God blesses people who give mercy to others, for they will be treated with mercy.

"God blesses people who have pure hearts. They will see God.

"God blesses people who work for peace. They will be called children of God.

"God blesses people who are treated badly for doing what is right. The Kingdom of Heaven will belong to them."

Jesus continued, "God blesses you when people make fun of you, do bad things to you, lie about you, and say bad things about you because you follow me. Be happy about it, because a reward is waiting for you in heaven. Remember that people did the same thing to the prophets who lived before you."

67
Jesus Feeds Many People

John 6:1-13

People followed Jesus wherever he went. They
wanted to hear him preach and see him do miracles
and heal the sick.

One day, Jesus climbed a hill with his disciples.
Jesus saw a big crowd headed their way. He asked
Philip, one of his disciples, "Philip, where can we buy
bread for all these people?" Although Jesus already
knew what he was going to do, he wanted to see what
Philip would say.

Philip replied, "Even if we worked for months,
we couldn't make enough money to feed all these
people!"

Another disciple, Andrew, spoke up. "There's a
young boy here with five loaves of bread and two
fish," he said. "But how will this be enough to feed
this many people?"

Jesus said to his disciples, "Tell everyone to sit down."

Jesus took the loaves of bread, thanked God for them, and passed them out to the people. He did the same thing with the fish. People started eating, and everyone had enough bread and fish. They all got full. When the people were done eating, Jesus told his disciples, "Collect the leftovers so nothing will go to waste." The disciples collected 12 baskets of leftover food. Jesus had fed more than five thousand people with one boy's lunch!

68

Jesus Walks on Water

Matthew 14:22-33

After feeding thousands of people, Jesus told his
disciples to take the boat to the other side of the lake
while he sent all the people home. When the crowd
was gone, Jesus went up on a mountain to be alone
and pray.

The disciples were far away from land when the wind
started to blow hard and the boat was tossed by waves.
Very late at night, Jesus walked toward them on the
water. The disciples trembled with fear when they saw
him. "It's a ghost!" they all cried out in terror. But Jesus
comforted them and said, "Don't be afraid. It's me."

Peter said to Jesus, "Lord, if it is really you, tell me
to come to you, walking on the water." Jesus said,
"Come!" Peter got out of the boat and started to walk on
the water toward Jesus. But when he saw the big
waves under his feet and felt the strong wind blowing
around him, he got frightened and started to sink.
"Save me, Lord!" he cried. Right away, Jesus reached
down and grabbed Peter's hand. "You have so little
faith," Jesus said. "Why did you doubt?" Jesus and
Peter both climbed into the boat, and then the wind
stopped blowing. After seeing everything that
happened, the disciples worshiped Jesus. They said to
him, "You really are the Son of God!"

69

The Transfiguration

Matthew 17:1-9; Luke 9:28-36

One day Jesus climbed up a mountain with his friends Peter, James, and John so they could pray, just the four of them. The disciples were tired and fell asleep. When they woke up they saw that Jesus' appearance had changed. His face was shining as bright as the sun, and his clothes were dazzling white. All of a sudden, the prophets Moses and Elijah appeared, and they stood talking to Jesus.

Peter said, "Master, it's good for us to be here. I'll make three shelters—one for you, one for Moses, and one for Elijah." Just then, a big cloud appeared and covered them. The disciples were terrified. A voice from the cloud said, "This is my dear Son, my Chosen One. Listen to him!" Suddenly, the disciples could only see Jesus. Moses and Elijah had disappeared.

When they came down from the mountain, Jesus told the disciples to keep quiet about what they had seen. "Don't tell anybody about what happened until the Son of Man has been raised from the dead," he said.

70

Who Will Be the Greatest?

Matthew 18:1-6

Once the disciples came up to Jesus and asked him, "Who is the greatest in the Kingdom of Heaven?" To answer their question, Jesus asked a little child to come close and stand among them.

He told his friends, "Here's the truth: unless you turn away from your sins and become like little children, you will never get in to the Kingdom of Heaven." Jesus continued, "Anyone who becomes humble like a little child is the greatest in the Kingdom of Heaven. And anyone who welcomes a little child like this one is also welcoming me."

Jesus told his disciples, "If anyone causes a little child who trusts in me to sin, it would be better for him to be dropped in the middle of the sea with a big stone tied around his neck."

71

The Farmer and the Seeds

Luke 8:4-15

Jesus told people stories with hidden meanings. These stories were called parables.

One time, Jesus told a parable about a farmer who went out to plant his seeds. He took big handfuls of seeds and threw them across the field. Some of the seeds fell on a path. People stepped on them and birds came and ate them. Some seeds fell on rocky ground where there was not a lot of soil. They grew quickly, but when the sun got hot, they dried up because they didn't have deep roots. Some seeds fell on thorns, and the thorns choked out the little plants. But some seeds fell on good soil. Those seeds produced a crop that was 100 times more than had been planted.

Later, Jesus' disciples asked him what the parable meant. Jesus explained, "The seeds are the Word of God. The seeds that fell on the path and were stepped on or eaten by birds are like what happens to people who hear God's message, but then the devil takes it away from their hearts. The seeds on rocky ground, which produced plants that dried up in the sun, are like the people who believe God's message with joy for a little while, but when troubles and hardships come,

their faith goes away too. The seeds that fell among the thorns describe people who hear God's message, but their faith is choked by worries, riches, or trying to live a comfortable life. And the seeds that fell on the good soil represent the people who hear God's Word, hold on to it, and have patience until they produce a big harvest."

72

The Good Samaritan

Luke 10:25-37

The teachers of Jewish law often listened to Jesus and tried to catch him making a mistake. One day, an expert in the religious law asked Jesus, "What should I do to have eternal life?" Jesus asked him back, "What does the law say? How do you read it?" The man answered, "You must love the Lord with all your heart, soul, strength, and mind. And you

must love your neighbor as yourself." Jesus said, "That is correct. Do this and you will live."

The man wanted to prove that he was already doing the right thing. He asked Jesus, "Who is my neighbor?" To answer the man, Jesus told a parable about a man who was traveling to the city of Jericho but was attacked by some thieves. They stole his clothes, beat him up, and left him for dead along the side of the road. While he was lying hurt by the road, a priest came by. When he saw the injured man, he didn't stop. Another man, a Temple assistant, also saw the wounded man, but he also just continued on his way.

Then a Samaritan came by. No one would expect him to stop and help the man, because Jews and Samaritans did not like each other. But he did stop. He used oil and wine to clean the man's wounds and wrapped them with bandages. He lifted the hurt man up on his donkey and took him to an inn, where he continued to take care of him. The next day, before he left, the Samaritan gave money to the innkeeper and said, "This is to pay for everything that he needs. Take care of him. If you have to spend more for him, I will repay you when I come again."

Jesus then asked the expert in the law, "So out of the three people who saw the hurt man, who do you think acted as a neighbor to him?" The religious expert replied, "The one who cared for him." Jesus told him, "Go and do the same."

73

The Good Shepherd

John 10:1-18

Jesus described himself as a good shepherd. He said, "Anyone who enters the sheep pen by any way other than the gate is a robber. The one who enters through the gate is the shepherd. The gatekeeper opens the gate for the shepherd, and the sheep listen to his voice. He calls all his sheep by name and leads them out to eat. The sheep follow him because they know his voice. I am the gate for the sheep. If anyone enters through me, he will be saved. A thief comes to steal, and to kill, and to destroy. My purpose is to give a life that is rich and meaningful."

Jesus continued, "I am the Good Shepherd, the kind who gives his life for the sheep. Someone who is not a shepherd will run away when he sees a wolf coming. He will do that because the sheep don't belong to him and he doesn't really care about them. But a shepherd will protect his sheep from the wolf.

"I am the Good Shepherd. I know my sheep and they know me. I have sheep that are not in the sheep pen. I will gather these sheep too, so that there will be one big flock under one shepherd. The Father loves me because I give my life so I can take it back again. I do this by my own choice. I can lay down my life and then take it back again. This is what the Father has asked me to do."

74

The Lost Son

Luke 15:11-32

Another time, Jesus told a parable about a man who had two sons. The younger of them told his father, "I want my inheritance now, before you die." The father agreed and divided his wealth between his two sons. The younger son moved to a faraway place. There he wasted all his money partying and making bad choices. When he had no more money left, he had to get a job feeding pigs. He said, "Back home, my father's servants are doing better than I am. They have a lot to eat while I'm here starving. I will go back to my father and tell him, 'I have sinned against God and against you. I don't deserve to be called your son anymore, but please accept me as your servant.'"

The younger son headed back to his father. He was still a long way from home when his father saw him coming and ran toward him. He threw his arms around his son and kissed him. The son told his father, "I have sinned against God and against you. I'm not worthy to be called your son anymore, but please accept me as your servant." But his father told his servants, "Get the best robe in the house and put it on my son. Get a ring for his finger and sandals for his feet. And kill the calf that we have been fattening. We will have a party. We will celebrate! My son was dead and now he is alive. He was lost, and now he is found."

The older son was working in the fields while this was happening. When he got home, he saw the party going on and learned that his younger brother had returned. The older brother became so angry that he wouldn't even go inside the house. His father came out to see what was wrong. The older son said to his father, "I have been working for you all these years. I did everything you wanted me to do, but you have never given me even a young goat so I could party with my friends. Now, what is this? Your son is back after wasting your money, and you kill the fattened calf to celebrate his return!"

The father said, "My dear son, you have always been with me, and everything I have is yours. But we have to celebrate, because your brother was dead, but now he's alive again. He was lost, and now he is found."

75

Ten Are Healed; One Is Thankful

Luke 17:11-19

Jesus was on his way to Jerusalem when he entered a village where 10 men were sick with leprosy, a terrible skin disease. When the men saw that Jesus was traveling through their village, they cried out to him from a distance, "Help us, Jesus! Help us!"

Jesus said to them, "Go and show yourselves to the priests!" They obeyed and started walking. As they went, they noticed how their skin began to clear up until there was no more sign of leprosy on their bodies anymore.

One of the men came running back to Jesus, shouting, "Praise God!" He bowed down at Jesus' feet, thanking him for what he had done. "Thank you,

Jesus! Thank you!" he said, over and over again. This thankful man was a Samaritan and not a Jew like the other lepers.

Jesus said, "I thought I healed 10 men. Where did the other nine go? Why did no one else give praise to God except this foreigner?" He then said to the man, "Get up and go. Your faith has healed you."

76

Lazarus Lives!

John 11:1-44

Jesus had three good friends who lived in the
town of Bethany: a man named Lazarus and his
sisters, Mary and Martha. One day Lazarus got very
sick. His sisters sent a message to Jesus to let him
know that his friend was sick. Even though Jesus
loved Lazarus very much, he stayed where he was for
two more days before going to see him.

When Jesus and his disciples arrived, Lazarus
was dead. He had already been in his grave for four
days. When Martha learned that Jesus was on his
way, she went to meet him, while Mary stayed in
the house. Martha said to Jesus, "If only you
had been here, my brother would still be alive.
But even now I know that God will give you
whatever you ask."

247

Jesus answered, "Your brother will rise again."

"I know he will rise with everyone else, at the resurrection," Martha said.

"I am the resurrection and the life," Jesus replied. "Anyone who believes in me will live even after dying. Everyone who lives in me and believes in me will never die. Martha, do you believe this?"

"Yes, Lord," Martha replied, "I have always believed that you are the Son of God." Martha then returned to Mary and told her that Jesus wanted to see her.

When Mary saw Jesus, she fell down at his feet and cried, "My brother would have not died if you had been here." She cried, and her friends and relatives who were with her cried too. This made Jesus very upset. He asked, "Where did you put him?"

"Lord, come and see," the people said. Then Jesus cried too. Some people said, "Jesus really loved Lazarus!" But other people said, "If Jesus was able to heal a blind man, then he could have kept Lazarus from dying!"

The tomb of Lazarus was a cave with a stone blocking the entrance. Jesus pointed to the stone and said, "Roll it aside." Jesus looked up to heaven and talked to God. He said, "Father, thank you for hearing me. I want to give the people standing here a reason to believe that you sent me." Jesus then said in a loud voice, "Lazarus, come out!" Lazarus walked out of the tomb with his hands and feet still wrapped in cloth. Jesus told the people, "Remove his grave clothes and let him go."

77

Jesus Blesses the Children

Mark 10:13-16

One day parents brought their little children to Jesus, asking him to put his hands on them and bless them. Jesus' disciples tried to stop the parents. "Don't bother Jesus," they scolded. "He is busy doing more important things."

When Jesus saw what was happening, he got angry with his disciples. "Let the children come to me," he said. "Don't try to stop them! The Kingdom of God belongs to the people who are like these children. Anyone who doesn't receive the Kingdom of God like a child won't be able to enter it."

Then Jesus took the children in his arms. He placed his hands on their heads and blessed them.

78

Jesus and Zacchaeus

Luke 19:1-10

One day Jesus traveled to the town of Jericho.
There was a man named Zacchaeus who lived there.
He was the chief tax collector of the whole region. He
was a very rich man, but he did not have any friends.
Everyone knew that Zacchaeus made himself rich by
charging people too much tax money.

When Zacchaeus learned that Jesus was passing
through his village, he said, "I have to see Jesus!"
There was a big crowd along the road waiting to see
Jesus as he passed by. Zacchaeus was very short,
and he couldn't see over all the people. So Zacchaeus
quickly ran to get ahead of the crowd and climbed up

a sycamore-fig tree beside the road. "I'll see Jesus pass by from up here," Zacchaeus thought.

When Jesus walked by the sycamore-fig tree, he looked up—right at Zacchaeus. "Zacchaeus! Come down," he said. "I will come to your home today and be your guest." Zacchaeus couldn't believe what he had heard. He scrambled down from the tree and led Jesus to his home. Zacchaeus was so happy, but not everybody was happy for him. The people who saw what happened grumbled, "Why would Jesus want to be with this thief?"

What they didn't know was that a big change was happening in the heart of Zacchaeus. He told Jesus, "Lord, I will give half of everything I have to the poor. If I have taken too much tax money from anyone, I will give that person back four times as much."

Jesus smiled and said, "Salvation has come to this home. This is why I have come: to seek and save those who are lost."

255

79

A Colt for the Lord

Matthew 21:1-5

Jesus and his disciples were going to Jerusalem. On their way, they came to the village of Bethphage. Jesus sent two disciples ahead and said, "As you enter the village, you will see a donkey tied up with its colt beside it. Untie them both and bring them to me. If anyone asks what you are doing, just tell them that the Lord needs the colt. The owner will let you take the animals."

Long ago, God had sent his people a message through his prophets. The message said, "Tell the people of Jerusalem, 'Look, your King comes to you. He is humble, riding on the colt of a donkey.'" Jesus was making the prophecy come true.

80

Jesus Enters Jerusalem

Matthew 21:6-11

Jesus and his disciples were about to enter
Jerusalem. The disciples had done what Jesus asked
and had brought the donkey and its colt to him. They
threw their coats over the colt for Jesus to sit on, and
Jesus rode the colt into the city.

There was a huge crowd of people waiting for
Jesus. Some people spread their coats on the road
ahead of him while other people cut down branches
from the trees and laid them on the road. They made
a big, happy parade for Jesus, treating him like a
king. The crowd shouted, "Praise God for the Son of
David! Blessings on the one who comes in the name
of the Lord! Praise God in highest heaven!"

The city was bursting with excitement. Some
people asked, "What is happening? Who is this man?"
Those who recognized Jesus said, "This is Jesus, the
prophet from Nazareth in Galilee."

81

The Last Supper

Matthew 26:17-35; Mark 14:12-31; Luke 22:7-34

It was almost time for the feast of Passover. Jesus wanted to share the Passover meal with his disciples, so he sent Peter and John ahead to Jerusalem to prepare the meal. "As soon as you enter the city," Jesus said, "You will see a man carrying a pitcher of water. Follow him. The house he enters is the place where you should prepare our Passover meal." Everything happened just as Jesus said, and the owner of the house led Peter and John to an upstairs room that had already been set up for them. So they got the meal ready.

When it was time to eat, Jesus and his disciples gathered around the table and sat down. Jesus said, "I have been looking forward to eating this Passover meal with you before my suffering begins. I won't have this meal again until we all eat it together in the Kingdom of God." During the meal, Jesus took some bread, thanked God for it, and broke it in pieces. He gave it to his disciples and said, "This is my body that is given for you. Eat this bread to remember me." After they finished their supper, Jesus took a cup of wine and thanked God for it. He passed the cup around to his disciples and said, "This cup is the new

covenant between God and his people, an agreement confirmed with my blood, poured out for you."

After this, they all headed out to the Mount of Olives. On the way, Jesus said to his disciples, "You will all leave me tonight."

Peter protested, "Everyone else might leave you, but I won't."

Jesus looked at Peter and answered, "Peter, before the rooster crows at dawn, you will say three times that you don't know me." But Peter said, "No! I would rather die than do that." The other disciples all said the same thing.

82

In the Garden

Matthew 26:36-56; Luke 22:39-48; John 18:1-9

Jesus and his disciples reached a grove of olive trees on the Mount of Olives, a garden called Gethsemane. It was a place they had often gone before. Jesus told most of his disciples to wait for him while he went to pray. He only brought Peter, James, and John with him farther into the garden.

Jesus was sad and upset. He said to the three

of them, "My heart is breaking. Stay here and pray with me."

Jesus walked even farther into the garden of Gethsemane while the three disciples stayed behind. He fell to the ground and prayed, "My Father, if it is possible, please take this cup of suffering from me. But do what you want, and not what I want."

After praying, Jesus went back to Peter, James, and John and found them asleep. He said to Peter, "Couldn't you stay awake and keep watch with me for an hour? Stay awake and pray that God will give you the strength to face temptation." Jesus left them again to be by himself. Again, he prayed, "My Father, if it is not possible for this cup to be taken away from me, then I pray that your will may be done."

When Jesus returned to where his disciples were, he found them sleeping again. Jesus left them a third time and prayed the same thing. An angel came to help him and gave him strength.

Jesus then went back to the disciples and told them, "It's time for me to be handed over to evil people. Get up! Let's go! I can see the man who has betrayed me."

While Jesus was still speaking, a group of men approached him. The group was led by Judas, one of the 12 disciples. He went over to Jesus and kissed him. He had agreed with the soldiers that he would kiss the man they were supposed to arrest. Jesus asked Judas, "Are you betraying the Son of Man with a kiss?" Jesus was then arrested and taken out of the garden. All the disciples ran away in fear.

83

Peter Denies Knowing Jesus

Matthew 26:57-58, 69-75; Mark 14:53-54, 66-72;

John 18:12-18, 25-27

The soldiers that arrested Jesus took him to the high priest's house. Peter followed at a distance and stood by the fire in the courtyard. He wanted to be close by to see what would happen to Jesus.

A servant girl recognized Peter and said, "I know

you. I've seen you with Jesus." But Peter lied, "I don't know what you are talking about."

A little while later another servant girl noticed Peter. "That man is friends with Jesus of Nazareth," she said, pointing at Peter. For the second time, he denied knowing Jesus. "I don't know the man," he said.

Later another group of people came up to Peter and said, "You must be one of the followers of Jesus. You talk just like them." Peter shouted, "Listen, I don't know him!" Right then, while Peter was still speaking, a rooster crowed.

Then Peter remembered what Jesus had said about him while they were sharing the Passover meal: "Before the rooster crows at dawn, you will say three times that you don't know me." Peter ran away, crying with shame and sadness.

84

Jesus Is Questioned by the Jewish Leaders

Matthew 26:59–66; 27:1, 11-14;

Mark 14:53-64; 15:1-5

Jesus was at the house of the high priest, where the chief priests and the Jewish leaders had gathered to ask him questions. They were looking for an excuse

to punish and kill Jesus, so they asked people to tell lies about him. Some men came and said, "We heard him say that he will destroy God's Temple and build another in three days."

The high priest stood up and asked Jesus, "Why don't you say anything to defend yourself?" But Jesus did not answer him. The high priest then asked, "Are you the Son of God, the Messiah?"

Jesus replied, "You have said it. Someday you will see me sitting at the right hand of God, and returning to earth in the clouds of heaven."

The high priest said, "What else do we need to hear? No need to listen to any more witnesses. You have heard him speak lies against God." The leaders proclaimed him guilty and sentenced him to death.

The next day, the men met again. They decided to send Jesus to the Roman governor, Pilate. They tied Jesus up and took him there. When Pilate saw Jesus, he asked, "Are you the king of the Jews?" Jesus replied, "You have said it." Pilate asked again, "Don't you hear the crimes they accuse you of? Why don't you defend yourself?" But Jesus refused to answer, which surprised Pilate very much.

85

Jesus before Pilate

Matthew 27:15-26; Mark 15:6-15; Luke 23:18-25;
John 19:13-16

At that time, it was the tradition that the Roman governor of the Jews would free one prisoner every Passover. The prisoner that would be freed was chosen by the people. At the time Jesus was on trial in front of Pilate, a man named Barabbas was also in prison. He was being punished for killing someone.

Pilate asked the crowd, "Who shall I set free? The murderer Barabbas or Jesus, the 'King of the Jews'?"

The chief priests told the crowd to demand that Barabbas be freed instead of Jesus. They all shouted, "Free Barabbas!"

Pilate then asked the crowd, "What shall I do with this man you call the King of the Jews?"

They all shouted back, "Crucify him!"

Pilate tried to change the people's minds and asked them, "What crime has he committed? What has he done wrong?"

But the crowd kept on shouting, "Crucify him!"

Pilate didn't think Jesus should be killed, but he was afraid the crowd would cause a riot and get him in trouble if he didn't give them what they wanted. Pilate took a bowl of water and washed his hands in front of all the people. He said, "This man's death is not my fault. It's your choice." He released Barabbas and ordered the soldiers to whip Jesus and take him to be crucified.

86

The Crucifixion

Matthew 27:27-54; Mark 15:16-39; Luke 23:26-47;
John 19:17-30

Pilate's soldiers took Jesus away. They made fun of him and twisted a crown of thorns that they put on his head while they knelt down and said, "Hail, King of the Jews!" They made him carry a heavy cross to a place called Golgotha, which means "the place of the skull." But Jesus was so badly hurt from being whipped that he couldn't carry the cross the whole way. The soldiers grabbed a man named Simon and made him carry the cross the rest of the way to Golgotha. There they nailed Jesus to the cross. Above his head Pilate posted a sign that said, "Jesus of Nazareth, King of the Jews."

After the soldiers nailed Jesus' hands and feet to the cross, they played dice to see which of them would get his clothes.

When people saw Jesus, they made fun of him and shouted insults. They said, "If you are really the Son of God, why can't you come down from the cross?" The high priests and religious leaders also made fun of him: "He saved others, so why can't he save himself? He says he is the King of Israel. We will believe him if he gets down from the cross now."

Two criminals were crucified with Jesus, one on each side of him. One of them joined the crowd in mocking Jesus. He said, "Aren't you supposed to be the Messiah? Why don't you save yourself and us, too?" But the man on Jesus' other side scolded the first criminal and said, "Don't you respect God now that you are about to die? We are getting what we deserve, but this man is innocent. He has done nothing wrong." He then turned to Jesus and said, "Please remember me, Jesus, when you are in your Kingdom." Jesus told him, "Today, you will be with me in paradise."

From noon to three o'clock, the sky turned dark. Jesus then called out in a loud voice, "My God, my God, why have you left me?" Then Jesus shouted again, saying, "It is finished." Jesus breathed his last breath while the earth shook. Many of those who saw what happened said, "He really was the Son of God!"

87

Jesus Is Buried

Matthew 27:57-66; Mark 15:43-47; Luke 23:50-55;
John 19:38-42

Joseph of Arimathea was a rich man and one of
Jesus' followers. When Jesus was dead, Joseph went
to Pilate and asked him if he could take Jesus' body
from the cross and bury it. Pilate agreed. Joseph took
the body, wrapped it in clean cloths and spices, and
put it in his own new tomb near a garden. A man
named Nicodemus helped Joseph bury Jesus. After
Jesus' body was placed in the tomb, a big stone was
pushed in front of the opening of the grave. Mary
Magdalene and another woman named Mary, who
were both followers of Jesus, watched the men put
Jesus' body in the tomb.

The high priests and religious leaders went to see
Pilate. They told him, "We heard that Jesus said that
in three days he would come back to life. Let's put
guards at the tomb so that his disciples won't be able
to steal the body and then tell everybody that he has
risen from the dead."

Pilate said, "Take some men and let them guard
the tomb. Go and secure it as best you can." The
religious leaders did as he said.

88
Jesus Lives!

Matthew 28:1-10; Mark 16:1-14;
Luke 24:1-11, 35-42; John 20:1-2, 11-29

Very early that Sunday morning, Mary Magdalene, the other Mary, and their friend Salome went to Jesus' tomb. The women had spices to put on Jesus' body. As they walked, they wondered how they would move the huge stone that had been put at the entrance of the tomb. But when they got there, they saw that the stone had already been moved away! They went inside the tomb and found an angel dressed in white. The women were surprised and afraid, but the angel said, "Don't worry. Why are you looking in a grave for someone who is alive? Jesus is not here. He has risen from the dead, just like he said. Go tell his disciples that Jesus is going ahead of you to Galilee. You will see him there." The women ran from the tomb and told the disciples about what they had heard and seen.

Later Mary Magdalene went back to the tomb. She was standing outside it, crying, when she saw a man who she thought was a gardener. "Dear woman, why are you crying?" the man asked her. "Who are you looking for?"

"Sir, if you have taken him away, tell me where he is, and I will go get him," Mary sobbed.

"Mary!" the man said. Then Mary realized that it was Jesus!

"Teacher!" she cried out with joy.

"Go tell my disciples that you have seen me," Jesus said. And that's exactly what Mary did.

For the next 40 days, Jesus showed himself to many of his followers. They ate with him and touched his hands, where the nails had been, so they knew he wasn't a ghost. They were so happy to see that Jesus was alive. The Son of God had risen from the dead.

89

The Miraculous
Catch of Fish

John 21:1-14

One evening Peter said to some of the other disciples, "I'm going fishing."

"We'll come too," they said. So off they went to the Sea of Galilee.

The disciples got in their boat and fished all night, but they did not catch a single fish. Early next morning they saw a man standing on the shore. The disciples couldn't see who he was. The man called out to them, "Have you caught any fish?"

"No," they shouted back. He said, "Throw out your net on the right-hand side. You'll get plenty of fish that way." The men did as they were told, and when they threw the net into the water, it filled up with fish. The net was so heavy with fish that the men could not pull it up into the boat.

John turned to Peter and shouted, "It's the Lord!" Peter was so excited that he jumped off the boat and swam toward the shore. The rest of the men stayed in the boat and pulled the net full of fish to the beach. That day they caught 153 large fish, but their net didn't break.

When the disciples reached the shore, they saw that Jesus had made a fire and was preparing some fish and bread for them. "Let's have breakfast!" Jesus said as he served the bread and fish to the men. They all saw that it really was Jesus.

90

Going Back to Heaven

Matthew 28:16-20; Mark 16:15-20; Luke 24:50-53;

Acts 1:6-11; 1 Corinthians 15:6

Jesus proved that he was alive by showing himself to many people. He kept teaching his followers, reminding them about God's Kingdom. There was even a time when he showed himself to more than 500 people at once!

Forty days after Jesus' resurrection, the 11 disciples went to the mountain in Galilee where Jesus had told them to go. They met Jesus there and worshiped him. He told the disciples, "I have been given all power in heaven and on earth. Go and teach people about me in every country. Baptize them in the name of the Father and of the Son and of the Holy Spirit. Teach these new disciples to obey everything I have taught you. I promise that I will be with you forever, even until the end of the world."

Now it was time for Jesus to go back to heaven. He lifted his hands to the sky and blessed his followers. As the crowd watched, Jesus rose toward heaven. He completely disappeared as he returned to the Father. Then two angels appeared. "Why are you looking up at heaven?" they asked. "Jesus will come back again in the same way he just went into heaven." Jesus' followers went back to Jerusalem, worshiping the Lord. Their hearts were overflowing with joy!

285

91

The Holy Spirit

Acts 2:1-41

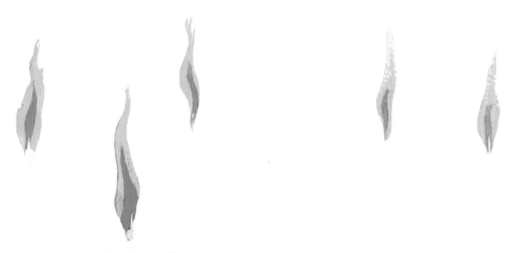

Before Jesus died, he told the disciples that he would send the Holy Spirit to guide them and give them comfort. Weeks after Jesus' death and resurrection, the Holy Spirit finally came. The disciples were meeting in a house when suddenly they heard the sound of a roaring wind. Then they saw what looked like little flames of fire land on people's heads. Everyone in the meeting was filled with the Holy Spirit. They began to speak in different languages. The Holy Spirit gave them the power to do this.

At the same time, many Jews who followed God were in Jerusalem for a religious celebration. They

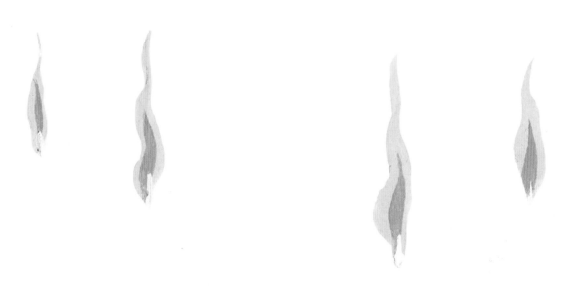

came from many different nations. They heard the sound of the roaring wind too, and they came running, wanting to see what was happening. When they saw the disciples, they were shocked to hear them speak in different languages. They said, "How can this be happening? These disciples are all from Galilee, but they're speaking to us in our own languages!" They were amazed to hear the disciples tell them about God's miracles and how God's Son came into the world to save people. Thousands of people decided to get baptized and follow Jesus that day!

92

Peter Heals a Lame Man

Acts 3:1-16

Peter and John were on their way to the Temple for the afternoon prayer meeting. At the gate there was a man who couldn't walk. He begged people for money every day. "Can you give some coins to a poor man?" the beggar asked Peter and John. Peter said, "I don't have silver or gold, but I will give you what I have. In the name of Jesus Christ, get up and walk!"

Peter took the man's hand and helped him up. Instantly the crippled man's feet and ankles grew strong. He was so happy that he started jumping up and down. Then he went with Peter and John into the Temple court to pray and thank God.

When the people saw the crippled man, they were amazed by what had happened to him. Peter said to the crowd, "Why are you surprised? This isn't something we can do by our own power. This can only be done in Jesus' name. Jesus is the one you handed over and had killed! You killed the one who gives life, but God raised him from the dead. John and I can tell you that we saw him alive after he was killed. This man in front of you has been healed because of his faith in Jesus. And that kind of faith can only come from God."

93
Brave Stephen
Acts 6:1–7:60

More and more people in Jerusalem decided to follow Jesus. A man named Stephen was chosen to help with the church. He was a man of faith and was filled with the Holy Spirit. With God's power, he did amazing miracles. But not everyone was happy with

him. Stephen's enemies brought in some men to lie about him. They said, "This man spoke out against the Temple and against the laws Moses gave us. He said that Jesus will destroy the Temple and change the way we've always done things."

When the religious leaders asked him about this, Stephen reminded them about all the things God had done, from the time of Abraham up to the time Jesus came. Stephen said, "You stubborn people! You have hard hearts. You are always fighting the Holy Spirit, and you won't listen to me. The leaders before you killed the prophets who told about Jesus' coming. Now you have turned against God's own Son."

The religious leaders got really angry when they heard Stephen's speech. But Stephen looked up into heaven and said, "I can see Jesus standing right beside God's throne."

The religious leaders grabbed Stephen and dragged him out of the city. As the men picked up stones to kill Stephen, he prayed, "Lord Jesus, bring me into your presence. Don't blame them for what they have done to me."

94
Saul Meets Jesus

Acts 9:1-19

Saul hated the followers of Jesus. He was ready to do whatever it took to get rid of them. The church was growing fast, and he wanted to put an end to it. He went to the religious leaders and got permission to put the followers of Jesus in prison.

When Saul was traveling to Damascus to arrest Christians, a bright light from heaven came shining

down on him. He fell to the ground. Then he heard a voice saying, "Saul, Saul! Why are you attacking me?"

"Who are you?" Saul asked.

The voice said, "I am Jesus, the one you are attacking. Get up and go into the city. Then you will find out what to do next."

Saul stood up. He opened his eyes, but he couldn't see anything. His friends guided him all the way to Damascus. For three days, he was blind. He didn't eat or drink anything.

There was a follower of Jesus in Damascus named Ananias. The Lord told him to go to the house where Saul was staying. Ananias didn't want to go. He said, "This man, Saul, has done many terrible things to your followers in Jerusalem. He has the power to arrest all of us who believe in you."

The Lord told him, "You have to go. I have chosen Saul to share my message with people." Ananias obeyed, and when he found Saul, he put his hands on him. Ananias said, "Jesus sent me to you. He will help you see again, and you will be filled with the Holy Spirit." Suddenly, something like scales fell from Saul's eyes, and he could see again. He got up and was baptized.

From that day on, Saul's life was changed. The man who once chased followers of Jesus was now a follower of Jesus himself. Later, when he became a missionary to other parts of the world, people started calling him by his Gentile name, Paul.

95

Peter Goes to Jail

Acts 12:1-17

The church kept getting bigger and bigger, but this only made some people angry. One of them was King Herod. He killed some Christians, and he arrested Jesus' disciple Peter. In prison, 16 soldiers guarded Peter. Herod planned to bring Peter out for a public trial, but the church didn't lose hope. They kept praying for his release.

The night before his trial, Peter was chained between two soldiers. There were also soldiers guarding the gate to make sure he didn't escape.

Peter woke up when he saw a bright light in the cell. An angel said, "Get up, and put on your clothes and shoes." Peter's chains fell off, and he got dressed quickly. Then the angel told him, "Put on your coat and follow me."

Peter followed the angel and walked out of the cell. While he was walking, he thought he was just dreaming. They went by the first and second guard posts, but no one saw them. Then they reached the gate leading to the city. It opened by itself. They passed through the gate and walked toward the street. Once Peter started walking down the street, the angel left him.

Peter couldn't believe what had just happened. "The Lord saved me by sending an angel!" he said.

He headed straight to Mary's home, where many Christians had gathered to pray. He knocked at the gate, and a girl named Rhoda answered. "Please let me in," Peter said. When Rhoda recognized Peter's voice, she was so excited that she ran back inside to tell everyone. But she forgot to open the gate. "Peter is outside!" she said. The people inside didn't believe her. "You've lost your mind," they said. But Rhoda was sure. "Peter is outside! He is outside!"

Peter kept knocking, and when they opened the door, everyone was surprised to see him. "Keep your voice down, and I'll tell you how the Lord helped me escape from prison," he said. After telling them the whole story, Peter headed to another place to preach God's message.

96

Paul and Silas in Prison

Acts 16:16-34

Paul and Silas were going to a prayer meeting when they met a slave girl. This girl had an evil spirit in her that could tell the future. Her masters made a lot of money on her fortune-telling. She followed Paul and Silas, shouting, "These men are servants of God. They are telling you how to be saved." Day after day she followed them wherever they went. One day Paul said to the demon inside her, "In the name of Jesus Christ, I command you to come out of her!" The demon obeyed and left her.

The slave girl's owners realized that they had just lost their way of making money through her. They took Paul and Silas to the city leaders. They said, "These men are causing trouble! They are telling us to change our ways, and we won't do it!" An angry crowd gathered around Paul and Silas so they couldn't escape. They beat Paul and Silas with wooden sticks and then threw Paul and Silas into prison.

But this didn't stop Paul and Silas from praising God. Around midnight, when they were praying and singing hymns, the ground began to shake. It was an earthquake! The doors of the jail opened, and all the prisoners' chains fell off. When the prison guard woke up, he saw that the prison doors were open, and he thought all the prisoners had escaped. He was about to kill himself when Paul shouted, "Don't kill yourself! We're all here!"

The prison guard ran to the dungeon, where Paul and Silas were. He fell down, shaking. "Tell me, what can I do to be saved?" Paul and Silas said, "Believe in the Lord Jesus Christ. If you do, you and your household will be saved." In the middle of the night, the prison guard washed their wounds and his family prepared a meal for them. Paul and Silas shared God's message with the guard and his family, and they were all baptized. God saved the guard's entire family!

97

Paul's Stormy Ride

Acts 27:1–28:1, 11

Even though the religious leaders told him not to, Paul kept talking about Jesus. So they had him arrested and sent to prison. His trial would take place in Rome, so Paul, along with some soldiers and other prisoners, boarded a ship.

The journey was slow and difficult. When they reached the island of Crete, Paul gave the crew a warning. "If we keep sailing, our trip is going to be a disaster. We will lose our belongings and put our lives in danger." But the soldiers ignored what he said and kept sailing.

At sea, the ship was caught in a heavy storm. The next day, while sailing on the stormy sea, the sailors started throwing their supplies overboard so the ship wouldn't sink. On the third day, they threw the ship's gear overboard. The storm continued for many days. The sun hid during the day; the stars never made an appearance at night.

After many days, Paul said, "You should have listened to me. But an angel of the Lord told me that none of us will drown. We will all be safe. But I can't say the same thing for the ship."

Days passed, and then Paul said, "We've been here for two weeks, and we haven't eaten anything. Let's eat, because we'll need our strength for when we're rescued." Paul thanked God for some bread and passed it around. There was enough food for everyone.

The next day, the ship hit a reef and started to break. The soldiers wanted to kill the prisoners so none could escape, but one of the officers stopped them. He wanted to save Paul. He ordered everyone who could swim to jump overboard and swim to the shore. Those who couldn't swim grabbed planks and floated to safety. Everyone made it to land, just as Paul had said. They stayed on the island of Malta for three months before they boarded another ship to Rome.

98
Paul in Rome

Acts 28:14-31

After Paul's long journey, he finally made it to
Rome. When he got there, other followers of Jesus
greeted him. Paul was under arrest for following
Jesus, but he was allowed to live by himself with
a soldier guarding him.

Not long after he arrived, Paul met with the Jewish leaders at his house. They said, "Tell us more about what you believe." Paul talked to them about the Kingdom of God. Some people listened to what he said, but others wouldn't believe. When those who didn't believe in Jesus started to argue with him, Paul said, "This is what the Holy Spirit said would happen. 'These people will listen with their ears, but they won't hear a word. They will look with their eyes, but they won't see a thing.'"

Paul did his best to share God's message with them, but not everyone was ready to listen. He said to those who didn't believe, "I've given God's special people a chance to believe. Now I will share the same message with everyone else. I know they will listen!"

For two years, Paul welcomed people into the house where he was staying. Every time visitors came, he talked to them about the Kingdom of God.

99

Paul Writes Letters

Romans 1:16; 3:23-26

Paul traveled all over, telling people about Jesus. He started some churches and encouraged people in other churches. He taught them important things about God's message. But he couldn't always be with them—especially after he was arrested for following Jesus. So he decided to share the Good News by writing letters.

In his letter to the Romans, he told the church there how he felt about sharing God's message. He said, "I'm not embarrassed to talk about the Good News. God has the power to save everyone who believes in him, the Jews first and then everyone else."

In his letters, Paul helped people understand more about God and answered their questions. He knew that some people thought they were better than everyone else. He showed them the truth—that all of us start out the same way. "Everyone has sinned. No one measures up to God's perfection." Then he explained how people can be saved. "God has given us the gift of his grace. That free gift makes us right with him. Jesus paid the price to set us free."

Paul ended up writing at least 13 letters. He wrote to different churches and groups of believers in places all around the world. He asked people he trusted to take the letters with them to share with the churches. They read those letters and then shared them with other people. These letters became part of the Bible, and we still read them today.

100

Heaven

Revelation 3:20; 7:9; 21:1-4

John, one of Jesus' disciples, was sent to an island called Patmos. He was a prisoner there because he followed Jesus. While he was on the island, God gave him a peek of what the future would be like. John wrote everything down and sent it to different churches.

In his writing, John told people how God will make everything right in the end. People might be sad and think that evil is winning because of all the bad things happening in the world. But it won't always be that way. John said that someday Jesus will come back and Satan will have to pay for all the evil he has done. Someday God will make everything new. He will create a new heaven and a new earth. God will live with his people. He will wipe away every tear from people's eyes. No one will feel pain, no one will be sad, and no one will die.

Jesus said, "I am here! I am knocking at the door of your heart. If you hear my voice and open the door, I will come in and be with you."

John wanted to tell everyone about this wonderful news: heaven is beautiful, and God has invited all of us to be with him in heaven. God has made a way for

us to be saved. Man or woman, boy or girl, rich or poor, people from every country and every language— anyone can go to heaven because of Jesus, who died and paid for the sins of the world. Isn't that the best news you've ever heard?